T0157112

STAY CALM

AND

CONTENT

NO MATTER WHAT LIFE
THROWS AT YOU

CAT WILLIAMS

authorHOUSE®

AuthorHouse™ UK
1663 Liberty Drive
Bloomington, IN 47403 USA
www.authorhouse.co.uk
Phone: 0800.197.4150

Published by AuthorHouse 07/02/2018

ISBN: 978-1-4772-3487-7 (sc)
ISBN: 978-1-4772-3488-4 (e)

Print information available on the last page.

This book is printed on acid-free paper.

Contents

FOREWORD TO THE SECOND EDITION:

I am sure many of you have seen the iconic British 'Keep Calm and Carry On' image which inspired the cover for this book. The original poster would have been displayed around the streets of the United Kingdom if the Nazis had managed to invade the British Isles during World War II. It was never put on public display but was found several decades later and has since been printed on merchandise and become recognised the world over.

I had a 'Keep Calm and Carry On' poster on my kitchen wall as I began to write this book during the winter of 2011 / 2012. My husband, a British Army Officer, was fighting on the front-line in Afghanistan. I was living amongst inspirational fellow Army wives, and working with awe-inspiring clients who were facing some of the greatest challenges of their lives. I was asking myself "What is the secret of keeping calm and carrying on no matter what our circumstances? Can we all learn to do it?"

I began to research the secrets of staying calm. I shared them with my clients, and as they in turn shared their inspirational stories with me, this book became the result.

As I write this forward to the second edition I am thankful for how far this book has brought me. I have been featured on nationwide television and radio shows and in newspapers and magazines, as well as recording a TEDx talk entitled

'Toilet Seat Therapy – what to do when you don't know what to do' which is on YouTube.

I continue my work as a relationship counsellor and give talks, presentations and workshops around the UK on the principles of resilience, emotional well-being and healthy relationships. I am thankful to all the individuals, schools and workplaces who have provided me with these opportunities to make a difference.

I hope you enjoy the book and I'd love to hear from you.

Best wishes, Cat.

www.staycalmandcontent.com
Blog – Interviews – Articles – Testimonials
Workshops - Presentations - Videos
Facebook: Stay Calm and Content
Twitter: @catstaycalm
YouTube: Stay Calm and Content

Introduction

If you picked up this book hoping for a straightforward way to feel happier and to get on better with the people in your life, then I believe you have found what you are looking for.

This book began as an approach I used during counselling sessions. Some of my clients encouraged me to publish my thoughts and ideas so other people might benefit from them. For reasons of confidentiality the stories in this book are fictional, but the positive changes that occur in the stories are similar to changes that have actually happened. An acquaintance who confided in me once said,

'Now that I understand myself better and have learnt how to feel okay no matter what, I have naturally become much calmer, and I make much better choices about how I react to stressful or difficult situations. The challenges that I still face on a daily basis sort themselves out much more quickly, now that I understand what generates my emotions, and therefore how I can manage them better. I have stopped making things worse by getting overly stressed, anxious, or annoyed at myself, or other people. I am much more content with life and feel much happier.'

Is there someone with whom you don't have a great relationship? You argue, don't speak much at all, or don't feel good in his or her company? I believe that person affects your self-esteem and that you could be affecting his or hers.

How it began . . .

I chose a book from our work library to help me with a particular client who had low self-esteem. The book's introduction described how people attend self-help groups for a variety of problems: depression, anxiety, obsession, alcoholism, eating problems, and so on. However, one line struck me as particularly important: 'I think I am coming to the conclusion that there is only one problem—and it's one that almost everyone shares: LOW SELF-ESTEEM' (Gael Lindenfield, *Self-Esteem*).

I thought about this line and about the vast spectrum of human experiences and challenges we might face, and I found myself agreeing that feelings of low self-esteem are not just experienced by *some* people, but that we can *all* feel low self-esteem at certain times, and we describe this in terms of negative emotions, such as stress, anxiety, anger, fear, jealousy, and so on.

Nathanial Branden described self-esteem as 'the sum of self-confidence (a feeling of personal capacity) and self-respect (a feeling of personal worth)'.

There are several definitions of self-esteem, but for the purpose of this book, I think that describing is as a combination of self-worth, self-respect, and self-confidence is the best definition. I feel that using the term 'self-esteem' is the most straightforward way to try to explain what makes us all 'tick'. If we can pick apart how our self-esteem has been constructed, how it affects our lives and the lives of others, and by what it is influenced, then we can learn to control it, and to stay calm and content no matter what life throws at us.

> 'Tell me how a person judges his or her self-esteem and I will tell you how that person operates at work, in love, in sex, in parenting, in every important aspect of existence—and how high he or she is likely to rise. The reputation you have with yourself—your self-esteem—is the single most important factor for a fulfilling life.'
> —Nathanial Branden

Staying calm and content is about self-esteem.

Emotions come from within us. We could all watch the same event, such as a wedding, and feel different about it—positive or negative—depending on our perspective. Emotions are created internally and not by external events or circumstances, which are neutral. As Shakespeare observed, 'There is nothing either good or bad but thinking makes it so' (Hamlet II, ii).

In other words, there are no positive or negative events unless they mean something to us and we choose to let them positively or negatively affect our self-worth, self-respect, or self-confidence.

Positive self-esteem

When we feel 'at our best' is when our self-esteem is good. When we are feeling good about ourselves we usually feel confident in our ability to cope with life, even under challenging circumstances, and we don't feel too sorry for ourselves. We accept and like ourselves, so we don't usually abuse our bodies with destructive habits or choices, such as drinking or eating too much, because we don't need to make ourselves feel better. We also generally accept other people and are considerate and kind because we don't need to judge, criticise, or take control of others to make ourselves feel better. We are more likely to forgive others if they make mistakes and to forgive ourselves too, because we are less likely to criticise ourselves for not being good enough.

Therefore, self-esteem is about accepting ourselves as good enough—but not perfect because no one is perfect. It is not about feeling self-important and better than other people but about having the opinion that 'I'm no better than anyone else, but no one is better than I am either'. This, in my opinion, is the 'secret to happiness' for which so many people in books, films, and real life search. The secret isn't 'out there'; it is within ourselves, and we all have the ability to find it.

> 'It is not easy to find happiness in ourselves,
> and it is not possible to find it elsewhere.'
> —Agnes Repplier

Another way of thinking about self-esteem is that it is the voice in our heads that asks questions like 'Do I feel okay right now?' 'Am I able to cope with this?' 'Will I feel okay as a person if I do or don't do this?'

No matter how confident, accomplished or successful we might appear on the outside, we all question ourselves. Some of the most outwardly successful and confident people can actually be highly self-critical and lacking in confidence in certain situations; they may have just learnt to hide these feelings from others in order to appear competent. Many important and famous people experience feelings of low self-esteem in certain areas of their lives, even though it might appear that they 'have everything'. Their self-worth and self-confidence might often depend on being successful and acceptable in the eyes of others; they might not always value or like themselves very much. Many people might try to control or escape from critical or negative feelings through addiction to drugs or alcohol, by controlling or criticising other people in their lives, or via self-abuse or obsessive control of eating or other habits.

> 'You have so much pain inside yourself that
> you try and hurt yourself on the outside
> because you want help'
> —Princess Diana

> 'For some reason, all artists have self-esteem
> issues.'
> —Whoopi Goldberg

I believe control of self-esteem lies behind the ability of some individuals to survive horrendous circumstances, unimaginable bereavement, or terrible crimes against themselves or their families and come out of those experiences with their faith in themselves intact. They do not allow those terrible circumstances or events to change how they feel about themselves.

> 'No one can make you feel inferior without
> your consent.'
> —Eleanor Roosevelt

Often, these brave individuals can also forgive their enemies because they take the view that their enemies 'know not what they do' or why they do it. In other words, their enemies have poor self-esteem and use evil actions to feel okay about themselves or to feel powerful or important.

> 'He that undervalues himself will undervalue
> others, and he that undervalues others will
> oppress them'
> —Johnson

Thankfully, most of us in the developed world do not have to face extreme circumstances such as war, famine, torture or false imprisonment, or lose our families and homes, but our self-esteem can still be tested every day by the day-to-day challenges we face. We can choose to feel okay about ourselves no matter what has happened to us, or we can choose not to. Choosing to feel okay might sound unrealistic if we have experienced loss, abuse, criticism, neglect, or violence, but no person or situation can change our internal view of ourselves without our consent.

Having said that, if we experience these negative situations or events in childhood, then feelings of low self-esteem might start at an age at which we cannot understand or challenge them, so they often stay with us for a long time—perhaps forever.

If all of us woke up tomorrow and took control of our self-esteem, we would all have decided to stop self-criticism and to value ourselves just as we are, to value the bodies we have, our minds and individual attributes, and what we spend our time doing. We are all equally human; we don't have to be perfect, as nobody is, and we are all 'good enough' just as we are. We may have made mistakes or treated other people badly, for which there is no excuse, but if we can understand why we thought what we did was the right thing to do at the time in terms of our own self-esteem—that is, what made us feel okay or better about ourselves at that moment—then we can start to understand how to control our feelings and behaviour in the future, so that we can be in better control of the choices we make. We can change and aim to be better or different if we want to, but first we have to accept ourselves as we are now, accept our past actions and decisions, and forgive ourselves for our mistakes if we feel we need to, so long as we are determined to take responsibility for our actions from now on.

'Whatever you are doing, love yourself for
doing it. Whatever you are feeling, love
yourself for feeling it.'
—Thaddeus Golas

'Blessed are they who heal us of self-despising.
Of all services which can be done to man, I
know of none more precious.'
—William Hale White

Our self-esteem is controlled by our brains.

We could be having a normal day when suddenly something 'negative' might happen to us, and we immediately feel a physiological response that we interpret as a negative emotion. This immediate reaction is due to our fight-or-flight instinct, which has been there for our protection throughout our evolution. However, now that most of us lead relatively safe lives, our fight-or-flight instinct reacts more to emotional, rather than physical, threats to our well-being.

The area in our brain called the amygdala forms and stores memories associated with emotional events, particularly 'threatening' ones. The amygdala sends impulses to the hypothalamus for activation of the sympathetic nervous system, creating a physical and hormonal response—that is, feelings and emotions. Our mouths might go dry, we might feel sweaty or have butterflies in our stomachs, and we will feel nervous, angry, anxious—basically 'threatened' in some way.

Because our brains can store memories, they can also react to those memories before we are consciously aware that they are doing so. If a current situation even vaguely reminds our amygdala of a previous threat, the amygdala triggers our nervous system, and we feel negative emotions—often even before we know why. Our brains are very good at warning and protecting us, but the brain acts so quickly that it can frequently be more unhelpful than it is helpful. This process is also why we are more likely to see negatives in our lives than positives; our brains have evolved to search mainly for threats. Because of this we might need to consciously look for the positives in our lives. The instinctive parts of our brains, which find negatives quickly, will not recognize that the positives probably vastly outweigh the negatives. (I first came across some of these ideas through the work of Larry Bilotta).

> 'What a wonderful life I've had! I only wish I'd
> realised it sooner.'
> —Colette

Have you ever instantly disliked someone you have only just met? Your brain has probably triggered a negative emotion that is due to previously formed negative memories of a similar person. Our logical 'adult' brain can override this immediate emotion once it starts to assess the reality of the situation (that this is a new person we have no reason to fear yet), but our fight-or-flight instinct will already have triggered a warning.

When we feel anger, annoyance, fear, stress, anxiety, jealousy, and other negative emotions, it is likely that our brains have searched for and found memories of past negative events that are similar to the current situation, so they have triggered warnings. We immediately feel the same emotions we did during the past events; our logical brains might be overwhelmed by these emotions, and we might not be able to 'think straight', so we might believe the emotions and react accordingly even though the current situation might not be a threat at all!

If we are unaware that threats to our self-esteem influence our emotions, then we will also be unaware that our subsequent actions are attempts to repair our self-esteem. We do what makes ourselves feel better in some way—maybe lash out at another person or do something to comfort ourselves—and then think, 'I don't know why I did that.'

All of us live moment . . . by moment . . . by moment . . .

We make decisions in the present moment, and if we see every decision we have made as being based on how our words or action made sense in terms of our self-esteem, then we can accept that we all make decisions that make sense to us at the time. Therefore, even if we ultimately regret what we do or say, it is pointless to blame and criticise ourselves too much because our self-esteem decided that it was the right thing to do at the time.

Being aware of what influences our self-esteem and improving our control of it will help us to make clearer decisions moment by moment. Thus, we may lead more positive lives and feel more content and happy. We will still feel unpleasant emotions; in fact, when we understand why we are feeling certain emotions, we might allow ourselves to accept them and to feel them more completely because we will be less frightened, confused, or overwhelmed by them. We will still feel them, but they will have less control over our subsequent thoughts, words, or actions.

'There are two ways to meet your life; you may refuse to care until indifference becomes a habit, a defensive armor, and you are safe— but bored. Or you can care greatly, and live greatly . . . '
—Dorothy Canfield Fisher

'Every new adjustment is a crisis in self-esteem.'
—Eric Hoffer

Self-esteem awareness and improvement

Your 'Self-esteem Timeline'

Write out or think through your life story so far in terms of your self-esteem, starting from when you were born. Put the positive things that have happened to you above a central line and the negative things below the line. When you have finished, can you see your self-esteem story and why you might currently feel as you do about yourself? How have the negative or positive events affected you and influenced your beliefs and feelings about yourself? Why did you see those past events as negatives or positives—that is, how did they affect your self-esteem at the time? Do you feel any different about them now? How have they affected the choices and decisions you have made? Think of the people who feature in your timeline and how they have affected your self-esteem. How do they affect you now? What do you think affects their self-esteem? How do you think you might affect their self-esteem?

The whole you: Your 'Self-esteem pie'

How do you choose to spend your time each day? What do you like to do? With whom do you like to be? These people and activities—whether they are 'healthy' pursuits or 'unhealthy' ones that you might regret later—all make you feel good because they raise your self-worth, self-respect, or self-confidence in some way. All of the decisions we make come back to our self-esteem: a small decision like taking a packed lunch to work rather than buying lunch can be influenced by a desire to feel good about saving money or eating healthily; a big decision like changing jobs or getting married can be influenced by what changes to our self-worth, self-confidence or self-respect the choice might bring. Because there seem to be more choices available today than ever, and because we may expect to 'have it all', we can easily become confused or unsure about what we should do, and we can be very self-critical when we feel later that we made the wrong decision.

Think of yourself as a pie-chart made up of many different segments. This is the 'whole you' because many influences make up who we are and why we think and feel as we do. Our self-esteem encompasses all our memories, the people and experiences in our lives, and how they have and do influence us. What do you think you need in order to feel okay? What do you like or value? Our culture, religion, society, parents, relatives, friends, colleagues, life experiences, and much more all contribute to what we believe matters and what makes us feel 'okay' as a person. These influences can determine the decisions we make and the things we want or feel we need. Some influences are obviously stronger than others, which ones are strongest for you?

Look at the list below, which contains some examples—the list could be endless—of what might make up our 'self-esteem pie': things we might need, want, or reach for when we feel good or bad, or occupations we might spend our time doing. If you don't feel you are happy, what do you think you are missing? Why do you believe that missing piece would be the key to feeling better about yourself?

Earning money	Wearing expensive clothes	Spending money
Being in a relationship	Social networking	Saving money
Feeling loved by partner	Being in control	Being in charge
Clean & tidy house	Eating the 'right' food	Pleasing other people
Liking our job	Exercising	Music
Being good at our job	Feeling loved by family	Bargain hunting
Having children	Feeling appreciated	Eating favourite foods
Owning a 'nice' car	Being well-educated	Playing sport
Taking care of others	Having a belief or religion	Playing online games
Having a pet	Feeling loved by friends	Being alone
Cooking & entertaining	Being a good parent	Being on a winning sports team
Being a certain clothing size	Going on nice holidays	Having well-behaved children
Supporting a sports team	Gambling & winning	Current affairs knowledge
Reading	Sex	Being in a club
Being good at a hobby	Smoking	Drinking alcohol
Making or repairing things	Being 'right'	Being physically strong
Feeling physically attractive	Getting drunk or high	Not arguing
Going out with friends	Being on holiday	Not wasting things
Having successful children	Owning expensive things	Feeling intelligent
Being busy	Feeling respected	Feeling important

Not 'missing out' on things	Being cuddled/kissed	Being bought presents
Buying presents for others	Having others take care of you	Hearing loving words
Spending time with friends	Being outdoors	Making things

Are any of the things in our lives 'too important'? That is, have we let them become too important in terms of our self-esteem? Do they sometimes take more financial, physical, or emotional investment than we can really afford? Does our need for them sometimes cause pain or hardship to the people who are close to us? Are some of them purely about meeting the expectations of other people?

Many of us feel we are not happy because we would like to have things in our lives that are not there—more money, a different job, a relationship, a child, a thinner body, a better house, and so on. Where do these expectations of 'happiness' come from? Friends? Parents? Society? Have we really decided for ourselves what we need and what matters in our lives? Have we asked ourselves whether we agree with the beliefs and values we have or whether we have simply picked them up from others and only think we want them for ourselves?

> 'If we'd only stop trying to be happy, we'd have a pretty good time.'
> —Edith Wharton

> 'Most folks are about as happy as they make up their minds to be.'
> —Abraham Lincoln

If we are aiming for unachievable goals, then we might never be happy because we may never achieve them—unless what we really like is the pursuit, rather than the goal itself. Striving constantly to be better or different can prevent us from being able to accept ourselves, accept others, and 'be happy'. We can choose to change or aim to be 'better' but it is best to do this after we have come to terms with who we are now. We were good enough when we were first born, before we 'achieved' anything. Is a person with 'everything' any more of a person than someone with 'nothing'? When we feel okay no matter what, we can look more carefully at the pleasurable things we choose to have in our lives, rather than needing them to feel okay.

> 'A person's worth is contingent upon who he is, not upon what he does, or how much he has. The worth of a person, or a thing, or an idea, is in being, not in doing, not in having.'
> —Alice Mary Hilton

> A person's worth in this world is estimated according to the value they put on themselves.
> —Jean De La Bruyere

Make changes to your 'pie'.

Look carefully at what makes up your 'self-esteem pie', at what parts of it you can control and which are out of your control. Remember this well-known prayer:

> '. . . grant me the serenity to accept the things I cannot change, the courage to change the

things I can, and the wisdom to know the
difference.'
—attributed to Reinhold Niebuhr

Your self-esteem will be more consistent if it relies more on things you can control than on things you cannot. It is good to have things in our lives that help us to maintain our self worth, self respect, and self confidence; they can be virtually anything, as long as other people are not harmed in their pursuit or achievement. Think carefully about what you can choose to have in your life and what will help you with your self-esteem. You will be benefiting yourself and others if you maintain your self-esteem and are therefore more frequently and consistently 'at your best'.

You are wonderful just as you are, and you always have been.

Take yourself back to when you were a baby. Look closely at yourself as that small person, and tell yourself that you are wonderful and that you have a unique body and mind. Tell yourself that you don't need to try to be perfect or anything other than you are in order to love yourself and be loved by others. Tell yourself that you will make mistakes as you grow up but that you can forgive yourself for those mistakes because you will always do what you believe to be right for your self-esteem at the time. Tell that little person that others will hurt you along the way but that you can forgive them because they will act in the way they believe to be right for themselves and won't usually be thinking of your hurt or pain—only their own. You hold the only key to being the best person you can be and feeling 'good enough' about yourself, rather than absorbing the negative messages that you perceive to come from others.

Instant self-esteem

I have found this technique to be useful anywhere and at any time, even under very difficult circumstances.

Close your eyes. Imagine that a warm, golden light begins to pour onto and into your head from above you and that it fills you up until it starts to pour out through your fingers and toes. You feel warm and bright, and you feel happy just because you are. You arrived at birth with this golden light within you; it is your self-worth. You are okay. Your challenge is to maintain this feeling deep within you, no matter what happens to you in life, and to know that nothing and no one can extinguish it.

What negatively affects your self-esteem?

What people, situations or activities do you avoid? Can you look carefully at how they affect your self-esteem? What emotions or physical sensations do you feel in these circumstances, why do you think you feel this way? When have you felt like this before? Are old memories replaying and making you feel the way you felt in the past, even if the circumstances are different? By using some of the techniques above, do you think you could change your experience of these challenging circumstances by maintaining control of your self-esteem whilst you are in them? Can you think of ways to improve your self-esteem in these circumstances, such as how you are dressed, who is with you, or how you have prepared for the situation?

What is really going on?

Is there a negative situation on your mind at the moment—perhaps a person in your family with whom you don't have a great relationship, a person at work or school, a neighbour, or someone in your social circle?

What emotions do you feel when you think about that situation and that person? I think one of the hardest but most important things we can do is to stop and ask ourselves how we are really feeling about a person or situation that is bothering us. It's not always as easy as it sounds to stop and really think about it.

Finding the true emotions that are working beneath the surface and admitting them to yourself creates a huge release of tension. The human body experiences the release of physical tension as a very pleasant experience, and when we admit a deeply held emotion about something, it can feel as good as any other release of tension. However, we should initially only admit these emotions to ourselves as they have the potential to cause great harm to the other people involved. It must be remembered that we are the ones responsible for the emotions we feel.

Here are some examples:

I feel like I hate my sister because I have never felt as good as she is, and it has felt like she has always needed to be right and I can never be right.

I am jealous of my colleague because, although we are supposed to be best friends, other people listen to him more than to me, and I always feel invisible when he is around.

I never felt truly loved by my parents, and I sometimes hate them for that.

I am still grieving for my loss, and I am so angry that I am left alone and left feeling like this. I don't know how I will ever feel okay without them, its not fair.

I hate her. I'm scared of him. I feel useless, stupid, ugly, inadequate, fat, awkward, too old, too young . . .

By admitting whatever it is we are really feeling, we release the tension in ourselves and can start the process of accepting ourselves and how we feel about situations.

Don't blame yourself for the emotions you have.

Remember, your brain has been trying to protect you by triggering these negative emotions and warning you of a 'threat'. You have a reason for feeling the way you do. How is your self-worth, self-respect or self-confidence being affected by this person or situation? Is past damage to your self-esteem replaying itself? Once you have asked yourself what your true emotions are and how a threat to your self-esteem has generated them, you can ask yourself whether you want to change how you feel. Do you want to be someone who hates his or her sibling, boss, mother, in-laws, neighbour, or friend? Do you want to be someone who is jealous, scared, angry, or anxious in a particular person's company? Is that person in control of how you feel in his or her company? Can he or she give you self-esteem or take it away, or are you in control of how you feel about yourself and, therefore, how you choose to speak and behave? Do you think you have been behaving negatively toward someone in order to feel better about yourself?

> 'Don't compromise yourself. You're all you've got.'
> —Janis Joplin

> 'I keep my ideals, because in spite of everything
> I still believe that people are really good at heart.'
> —Anne Frank

You may be able to avoid particular people or situations, but if you can't avoid them, do you want to feel better in their company? It is easy to control how we feel with people we love and trust; if a person we like says or does something that could be interpreted negatively, we probably dismiss it as not meaning much or as something we have misinterpreted. However, if someone we already feel uncomfortable with says or does the same thing, then we find it much harder to control our reactions because we may feel threatened. The challenge of self-esteem is to control it amongst those people we 'don't like'; after all, controlling our self-esteem amongst our kind and trusted friends isn't much of a challenge!

Can anyone *make* you feel anything you don't want to feel? Can you begin to consider the other person's self-esteem and help them to feel more positive about you and himself or herself? If you could do this, how do you think the other person's reactions and behaviour toward you would change? Even if the other person didn't change, would you care as much about the situation if you had already taken control of how you feel in his or her company and thereby reduced the power you give him or her over your emotions?

> 'The most important skill in staying calm is not to lose sleep over small issues. The second most important skill is to be able to view all issues as small issues.'
> —Paul Wilson

Self-esteem in pictures

1)   'Fit your own oxygen mask before helping others.'

Once we have looked at everything we choose to have in our lives to help us feel okay, we can take responsibility for 'fitting our own oxygen mask'—that is, valuing ourselves enough to make time for what helps us with our self-esteem so we can then positively love and support others, rather than using or 'needing' them to feel better about ourselves.

When did you last feel 'at your best'—loved, successful, peaceful, happy? Imagine that time now and notice the positive effect it has on your current emotions. How could you help yourself to feel that way more often? What makes up your self-esteem 'oxygen' and what steps can you take straightaway to provide it for yourself.

2)   A tree

Imagine yourself as a tree. In order to survive the 'bad weather' of life, we need strong roots to stop us being blown over. The nurture and love we receive in childhood develops our 'roots', so if we didn't feel loved or nurtured enough, it might be like we have under-nourished roots. We might look like a strong, healthy tree on the outside, and the world might think we are 'fine', but if our childhood was not as enriching as it might have been, then there is greater potential for something to come along and 'knock us over'.

In fact, many of us didn't feel sufficiently nurtured or loved in childhood, but it is never too late to enrich our roots. The child we were is still within us, and we can nurture that child now by being kinder and more loving to ourselves so our roots can be strengthened and we can become a stronger tree that other trees can potentially lean on.

3) *A boat*

I also find it helpful to describe having good self-esteem as having a strong and well-maintained 'boat'. Life is like the uncontrollable sea and weather. Imagine that your boat contains yourself and the people you love and are responsible for. Only you can keep the boat strong enough to carry you all, and you are responsible for the direction in which it moves. Some people in the boat might help you, some might hinder you, but you are ultimately in charge of your own boat—that is, your self-esteem. The sea and weather (life) are unpredictable, so the best you can do is to prepare for change and unpredictability by keeping your self-esteem strong and by staying as well in control of it as possible. No one can control the weather—it will always change—but we can control ourselves.

If there are people in your life who are damaging your boat or trying to sink it, then think carefully about what to do about this. You cannot protect yourself or those you love if your boat is damaged and a storm comes along; you might fall out or sink, and those who you love and are responsible for might sink with you. How can you keep your boat strong?

We use many 'water-based' expressions to describe life's challenges, which is why thinking of our self-esteem as a boat can be a helpful analogy. Consider these everyday expressions:

Feeling 'all at sea'—Our self-esteem boat might be okay, but we don't feel in control of where it is going.

'Rocking the boat'—Someone or something is affecting our self-esteem and making us feel vulnerable to being 'tipped over'.

'Just keeping our heads above water'—We feel we have fallen out of our boat and don't feel great, but we are not quite drowning yet.

'Sinking the boat'—Someone—even we ourselves—destroys our boat and we sink. When we *'hit rock bottom'*, we hope we come up again and begin to build a new boat.

Use your imagination.

When our brains trigger negative emotional responses, they are often responding to our memories of a previous threat, rather than to the reality of what is occurring. We can learn to improve our control over our nervous systems and emotions by using our brains' power of memory and imagination.

We don't realise how much our imaginations rule our day-to-day lives. Has your mouth ever watered when you thought about your favourite food? Have you ever recalled a previous argument and become just as angry as you were when you had it? Have you ever watched a scary movie and then been scared in your own house afterwards? We use our imaginations all the time, and our brains and nervous systems respond as if what we are imagining were happening in real time.

When we know we will be facing something that could lower our self-confidence or self-worth, the best way to prepare ourselves and maintain our self-esteem is to use our imaginations. (Sports figures often do this.) We need to replace negative pictures with ones that will be helpful, rather than detrimental, in our current situation.

> 'If you think you can, you can. And if you
> think you can't, you're right.'
> —Mary Kay Ash

Imagine yourself at a time when you felt at your best—perhaps when you achieved something for which you had worked hard, or a day when you were participating in something you really enjoyed. It should be a time when you remember feeling good about yourself, your qualities, and accomplishments, or a time when you felt cared for by those around you and caring toward them. Focus on a moment from that memory and try to put yourself back in that moment when you felt at your best. Use your five senses to recreate that memory vividly. What did you see? What did you hear? What did you feel? What did you taste? What did you smell? Write this wonderful memory down—every little detail—and memorize it. Don't let negative thoughts in! Don't start thinking, 'Yes, but after that, someone criticised me and . . .' This is about your positive memory of feeling *at your best,* without negative thoughts. Our brains are structured to pick up threats more readily than the positive memories of life, so we have to *choose* to remember the positives.

If you want to feel more positive about certain people in your life, such as your partner, your mother, or your father, you can also practice remembering times when *they* were at their best, which will help you to remember that they have sometimes behaved well toward you even though they might not be behaving kindly at the moment—probably because of their own low self-esteem, or yours, which is altering your perception of them. Write a list of wonderful memories about your positive experiences with others.

The next time something happens in your life that you find upsetting, instead of letting it damage your self-esteem and cause you to be stressed, anxious, or angry, tell yourself that your brain is just finding a similarity between the situation and something that happened before; the 'threat' that is upsetting you might not be a real threat. Try to immediately replace the negative self-esteem memory with the positive self-esteem memory you have been practicing recalling in your imagination. Then your body will react accordingly and you will feel relaxed and positive. Taking this approach can be difficult for those who have had considerable unhappiness in their lives and who have more unhappy than happy memories, but feeling calm and content depends on the pictures that are currently in our imaginations. When we practice reliving our positive self-esteem memories, such positive thoughts can become our natural reaction when something challenging happens, and they can help us to maintain good self-esteem and remain calm, no matter what life throws at us.

Treat others as you wish to be treated.

Once you have taken charge of your imagination (and, therefore, your self-esteem), you might notice that other people begin to respond more positively toward you—probably because you are not threatening their self-esteem as much as you might have been before. Other people can see and interpret us in ways of which we are not even aware. We don't see the facial expressions they see, or how our body-language looks, or hear how our voice sounds to them. When we see threats everywhere our body language transmits fear and negativity, and others are more likely to feel threatened and respond negatively toward us; but when we focus on positive memories of ourselves and others our whole body language will change, and we are likely to make others feel more positive about themselves, and toward us.

'Happiness is good health and a bad memory.'
—Ingrid Bergman
'Don't wait for people to be friendly.
Show them how.'
— Anonymous

Internal Counsellor

Spend some time talking out loud to yourself and being your own self-esteem counsellor. Ask yourself how your day or week has been, how you are feeling right now, and why you think you are feeling that way. Ask what has positively or negatively affected your self-esteem recently, what emotions certain events caused you, and how you handled them. Remember not to criticise yourself, or others, but aim instead to understand what happened. Think about the coming days or weeks, what is worrying you right now, and why. Think about the people in your life, what might be going on with their self-esteem at the moment, how are their feelings or behaviour affecting you? How could you positively affect them and yourself this week?

You might feel strange talking to yourself out loud, but you will get used to it after a while and will enjoy your time with yourself!

First thing in the morning, last thing at night, and everything in between.

Have you ever awakened in the morning and wondered whether you can handle the challenges of the day ahead, or lain awake at night worrying about what tomorrow might bring? Staying calm and taking charge of your self-esteem can be as simple as saying to yourself something like, 'I'm not perfect, but I can handle anything because I can choose how I respond to it. I'm okay; no matter what happens, no one else can make me feel or behave in a way that I don't want to feel or behave. I don't need to be unkind to others; I can treat them with understanding and respect, even if they do not treat me that way.'

Saying this kind of thing first thing in the morning, last thing at night, and frequently throughout the day, especially when you feel your self-esteem might be at risk, is simple but can be effective.

Changing Ourselves

Changing ourselves can be difficult, whether it is how we think about ourselves or how we behave. Think about the diets we have tried, the new exercise regimes we were going to undertake, or the new habits we were hoping to create that would 'change our lives'. We usually revert pretty quickly to how we were living before, and then we might criticise ourselves because we didn't have the strength or willpower to persevere.

Taking charge of our self-esteem and stopping our criticism of ourselves and others can be like anything else; it can be easy to slip back into old ways of thinking and behaving because they feel normal and natural to us, even if we don't like them! It is hard to switch off an inner critical voice if it has been there since childhood, telling us that we aren't really good enough.

Portia Nelson's poem, 'Autobiography in Five Short Chapters', describes how trying to change ourselves can feel. Low self-esteem, critical thoughts, and the behaviour that might result from them can be like a hole in the sidewalk into which we keep falling, but we can all learn gradually to walk down a different street.

'The most beautiful people we have known
are those who have known defeat, known
suffering, known struggle, known loss, and
have found their way out of the depths. These
persons have an appreciation, a sensitivity, and
an understanding of life that fills them with
compassion, gentleness, and a deep, loving
concern. Beautiful people do not just happen.'
—Elisabeth Kübler-Ross

'It's only when we truly know and understand
that we have a limited time on earth—and
that we have no way of knowing when our
time is up, we will then begin to live each day
to the fullest, as if it was the only one we had.'
—Elisabeth Kübler-Ross

Get help

If we are finding it hard to increase and maintain our
self-esteem by ourselves, for whatever reason, then we must
get help. If we choose to get support it shows great strength
and courage, and that we believe in our own self-worth. The
people in our lives who might rely on us, need us to be okay
so we can help and support them. It is our responsibility to
seek help when we need it.

'To the world you may be just one person, but
to one person you may be the world.'
—Brandi Snyder

Such help could be from trusted friends or family, from
mental health professionals, or from a qualified counsellor

or psychotherapist. Choose someone who helps you to feel comfortable, safe, and supported and who listens carefully to you and focuses on the things with which you need their support. Be careful of being labelled as having a particular mental health condition; you are an individual with an individual life story and individual needs, if you are feeling that you are being seen purely as a 'condition', then you might not be getting the individual support you deserve.

'Adversity and perseverance and all these
things can shape you.
They can give you a value and a self-esteem
that is priceless.'
—Scott Hamilton

CRITICISM

Jenny

Every time my in-laws were due to visit I felt anxious because of the pressure I felt to have my house perfect and my children well-behaved and to cook lovely meals and so on. My mother-in-law, Marion, judged and criticised almost everything I did, and I just couldn't be myself around her. I was finding three children very hard work, and sometimes I wished I could go back to work part time just to have a break and to feel better about myself; but she would just tell me how lucky I was not to have to work and how she had enjoyed staying at home, then she would say that she was worried about how stressed my husband was looking, and she seemed to imply that I should be taking better care of him!

As I became more anxious and less and less myself around her, I started feeling more and more annoyed and angry that she made me feel this way. It started to cause problems with my husband. We tried to talk about it, but he would say, 'That's just the way she is, she had a different life from yours, so don't compare yourself.' This would just make me feel worse, I felt I should be more content to be a stay-at-home mum, like she had been content to be. Things got worse and worse, and I ended up feeling very depressed and just unable to cope with everything. I went to my GP and was put on anti-depressants and referred for some counselling sessions.

Once I began to look at my own self-esteem, my thoughts on my situation began to change. I realised that I was feeling criticised by Marion before she even arrived, and this was to do with my own feelings of self-esteem, as a mother. Because I questioned and criticised myself about whether I was a good mother or not and whether I should want to go back to work, it made me hear criticism from Marion, no matter what she said. She had more ability to make me feel criticised because I was already comparing myself to her, and I cared what she thought of me. I realised that, when she asked something like, 'When will you potty-train Eleanor?' I interpreted it as meaning, 'Why haven't you done it yet?' that is, a criticism. I even interpreted her motherly concern for her son as a criticism of me because I took it to imply that it was my fault he was stressed!

Once I realised that I, not she, was in control of my self-esteem, I realised that I had been largely inventing her judgment and criticism based on my interpretation of her words and behaviour. I thought carefully about my self-worth, self-respect, and self-confidence and realised that I was struggling within myself to feel 'good enough' as a mother and to value how well I was doing. My thoughts on going back to work were mainly to increase my self-esteem because I felt frustrated with the day-to-day tasks of mothering small children and wanted something to raise my sense of self-worth. I decided that increasing my self-esteem through work would be a good thing overall, it was important to me, and that was okay. I began to look at part-time options. I also realised I had been too proud to ask for enough help, so I asked my husband and family whether they could baby-sit so I could find time for exercise classes and meeting friends more often because I had let these things slip away.

Once I looked at Marion differently and tried to see her as an individual with her own self-esteem story, I realised that she probably felt low self-esteem around me, too, because she probably felt criticised and misunderstood when I was sharp with her and defensive. I talked to my husband about her life, and I learnt that she had qualified as a nurse before becoming pregnant with his elder sister, and she had never worked. I started to appreciate that Marion might actually be envious of the choices I have, and might be defending having been a stay-at-home mum because she felt forced to make that choice and needed to believe that it had been the right one.

Once I realised I didn't have to feel criticised by her because I, not she, had been judging and criticising myself, I relaxed in her company and stopped judging her or feeling critical of her, and I focused on getting to know her instead. I now like her as a person and don't react to her as 'the mother-in-law', which is a term that seems to imply criticism before you even know anything about the person! I have started explaining my point of view to her a little more, and she seems to be relaxing in my company now that I am not so defensive. I can tell my husband and father-in-law are glad we are getting on better, and all because I stopped and looked at the impact my own self-esteem was having on our relationship and decided to take control of it.

I wish we could stop all criticism of ourselves and others. This goal might sound ridiculous and unrealistic, but criticism implies someone should have behaved differently, and yet no one else can know for certain *why* someone says or does a certain thing at a certain moment.

*Don't judge anyone until you have walked a mile
in their shoes.*

Our self-esteem drives our thoughts and actions moment by moment, so unless we know exactly how another person felt in the moment they made a decision, we cannot decide that it was wrong in terms of their self-esteem at that time. Of course, we do not have to agree with or condone their actions, and there is no justification for abusing, degrading, controlling, or deliberately hurting other people, but people do things for a reason; they are doing what their self-esteem is telling them they need to do at the time. Unfortunately, however, negative self-esteem can sometimes cause negative actions against others if we seek to make ourselves feel stronger, better, or more in control.

> *There is always a 'reason' even if that reason is not a good one from someone else's point of view.*

Have you ever felt criticised? Have you ever criticised someone else? Feeling criticised can affect our self-esteem, but our decision to criticise others also comes from our self-esteem because we feel better about ourselves when we criticise others.

> 'When you judge another, you do not define them. You define yourself.'
> — Wayne Dyer

We most often notice and dislike things in other people that we don't like in ourselves; for example, if we don't like feeling angry, then we criticise others for being angry, and if we don't like being late, we criticise other people for being late.

'The passion for setting people right is in itself
an afflictive disease.'
—Marianne Moore

If someone criticises you, they are doing it to feel better about themselves, so we can choose not to feel criticised by them at all! Their reasons for criticising you have to do with their own self-esteem and need to make themselves feel better at that moment, so you don't need to believe their criticism and let it negatively affect your self-esteem.

'People are like sharks; they only usually attack
when they feel attacked.'
—from the film, *Couples Retreat*.

What often happens when we are criticised is that we feel the need to defend ourselves by criticising in return, which in turn damages the other person's self-esteem and increases the likelihood that they will criticise us back to make themselves feel better, and on and on and round and round.

However, taking charge of our own self-esteem can stop this cycle because if we can recognise that someone else is criticising us because they are experiencing low self-esteem, we can choose not to criticise them back and instead can aim to improve their self-esteem, aiming to create a win-win rather than a lose-lose situation.

Having said that, it is important to recognise that we can control only our own self-esteem, not anyone else's. We can try to understand others, see things from their point of view, and put their needs first, but we can never inhabit their inner world. Therefore, although our good deeds toward others might improve our self-esteem, we have no control over whether we are helping someone else's internal emotions, only they can control what they think about themselves. We can only try to have a positive influence and hope to have a positive effect.

Familiarity can breed contempt.

We often end up criticising the most those to whom we are closest and whom we love the most, or those by whom we most wish to feel loved. How many of us have felt criticised by our parents, our spouse, or our children? How many of us criticise them back or criticise ourselves because of what they say? Because the opinion of those we care about matters most to us we are more sensitive to their words and behaviour. Our close friends and relatives can influence our self-esteem far more than a stranger in the street can. Do you hear criticism from those closest to you and do you criticise them in return in order to feel better about yourself?

> 'A hurtful act is the transference to others of
> the degradation which we bear on ourselves.'
> —Simone Weil

Don't we want to be accepted, loved, and cherished by those closest to us? We want to 'be ourselves', to be accepted just as we are, and to be loved unconditionally. If we don't feel like this, then we must work first on valuing and loving ourselves and stopping our self-criticism. Only after we have climbed this mountain can we try to show unconditional love and acceptance to other people so they are less likely to criticise us or others in order to feel better about themselves.

Criticism might not be there at all.

When we feel negative about ourselves and have low self-esteem, it is easy to hear criticism anywhere and everywhere and to interpret virtually anything in a negative way. 'Have you started dinner yet?' is a harmless question, but it can be heard as 'You should have started dinner by now, so why haven't you?' Have you been guilty of hearing criticism that probably isn't there? I know I have!

If we are constantly interpreting events and people in a negative way—'they don't like me, they criticised me, they insulted me, they ignored me, they were rude to me . . .'—then it is probably time to ask why we are feeling so negative about ourselves, which is making us see everything in such negative terms.

Love for ourselves and others must be unconditional—that is, loving and accepting ourselves and each other just as we are, without criticism. When we show unconditional love to others, I believe we will receive it in return.

Childhood

Many feelings of low self-worth, low self-respect, or low self-confidence come from childhood, which is why it is so hard to recognise these feelings and make them go away. Our parents or those who cared for us during our childhood often have the greatest and most lasting influence on our self-esteem. Did you feel unconditionally loved by those who brought you up? How much did you feel criticised, neglected, or expected to be better or different?

As children, we are likely to take the opinion of others as fact because we are too young to analyse whether they are right or not. We assume that if our fathers, mothers, caregivers, teachers, siblings, or others close to us think we aren't good enough or should be different, they must be right. When we are adults, it can be difficult to challenge the beliefs we have held about ourselves since childhood, but it can be done.

> 'Praise is like sunshine to the human spirit; we cannot flower and grow without it.'
> — Jess Lair

William

I had what I have always described as a happy childhood. I was fed and clothed well, we went on holidays, and my parents helped me with my homework—all the usual things. My parents didn't actually express love very well though, they worried about me and wanted me to do well, so I think they did love me in their own way, but I don't remember feeling 100% sure.

When I had my own children, I started to struggle with disciplining them, and I found myself getting really annoyed with them when they wouldn't do as they were told. I kept thinking that a good father was one whose children did as he said, so I felt I must be a bad father, and I started to shout more in order to try to grasp more control. I criticised them for not getting dressed quickly by themselves, not sitting quietly at the table, not tidying up their toys quickly, or making a mess. Then when they were 'good', and I could see what lovely little people they were, I would feel annoyed and critical of myself for getting so cross with them when they were just children and I knew that they should be shown love at all times. I didn't know how to 'get it right' and be a good father, I thought other people were doing a better job than me and that I was trying hard but still failing. The more I tried, the angrier I got with myself and them.

One day I realised that I was going about things in an unhelpful way, and I thought about my own childhood. I realised that I hadn't really felt accepted or loved by my parents. I had felt criticised and never quite good enough, and I was repeating that pattern with my own children by criticising them and trying to make them what I thought they should be, rather than loving them just for who they are.

When I realised this, I also realised what I had to do. I had to show them unconditional love and find a way to teach them manners and right and wrong without criticising them for being themselves. I realised I could cuddle my son and say, 'I know you're a generous boy and you can share nicely with your brother,' rather than accusing him of being horrible and selfish and smacking him when he fought with him. I imagined writing a letter to my parents when I had been a child, and then I realised that it would probably be the same letter my children would like to write to me, and something which most people would like to write, no matter what age they are or who their parents are.

Dear Mum and Dad,

Please don't criticise me, ignore me, or imply that I am naughty, lazy, or not good enough, because I don't want to feel that way about myself. Please love me just for myself and help me to see the good in myself and the good in other people so I don't get so hurt by other people but can come to understand that they are sensitive too and will have reasons for their behaviour that won't be because of me.

Please don't favour my brother or sister over me, because it makes me feel like you think they are better than I; surely, I am worth the same as they are. When I am naughty or don't do as you ask, please recognise that I might just be doing the things that come naturally for a person my age and that I am not an adult who is deliberately disobeying and trying to annoy you. I need you to love me just as I am because you are my parents, and I don't have anyone else who can show me love like you can. Please recognise that, when I misbehave, I might just be seeking your attention, rather than feeling ignored; I want your love and acceptance, most of all, not your anger, but sometimes anger shows you care more than no reaction at all does.

Please teach me how to handle the emotions I feel. I feel anger, fear, envy, love, jealousy, and many other emotions, just like you do. When you feel these emotions, it helps me to see you experience them, but please try not to direct them at me. If you can explain afterward what you were feeling and why, then it will help me to understand where emotions come from and that they are normal and I can understand and manage them, rather than being overwhelmed by them. If you can manage emotions, then I know I can learn to.

If you argue with each other, please understand that it makes me feel that it is my fault because you often argue about 'the children', and you shout in front of us. I want you both to be happy because I worry that, if you argue, then you might split up. Then I will feel like it is my fault because maybe I'm not well-behaved enough, and I should have tried harder to be better or different so you didn't argue as much. I want you to stay together because that feels safe for me, and I don't want either of you to leave me.

I have heard it said that 'children need love most when they deserve it the least.' I think this is true because sometimes, when you shout at me, I don't understand what I have done wrong. I am only a child, and I can do only what feels right to me at the time. I like to show off to my friends sometimes so they will like me more, but this makes you really cross. I don't want to do anything that would make you stop loving me, so if I have done something you really disapprove of, or that seems horrible to you, then I promise I was not wanting to cause you not to love me.

Please find a way to teach me right and wrong whilst letting me know that you love me just because I am myself. Most of the time, I think you would love me more if I were better or different, but I don't always know how to please you and to be what you want me to be.

I need your help to figure out how to like myself and how to accept other people and cope with life, no matter what it brings, please help me.

With love,

Your Son

After writing this imaginary letter, I realised that I felt no blame toward my parents because I am sure they would have wanted me to feel loved and they wouldn't have realised that I didn't always feel it. I don't think they received enough love from their own parents, so they were doing their best to show me love at the time. They criticised me because they thought it was the best way to 'make me better', so I think, to them, their criticism meant they were showing concern and love for me. If I want to feel the warmth and affection that I didn't feel as a child, then I need to find a way of gaining that now, as an adult, so I can improve my own self-esteem and be a kinder and more loving father to my children and a more loving and accepting partner to my wife.

Communication, Arguments and Battles of the Sexes

Everyone agrees that communication is essential for good relationships, but what exactly is good communication?

I describe good communication as being able to explain clearly to someone else what is going on with our self-esteem, rather than communicating the raw emotions we might be feeling. Good communication also requires trying to understand what is going on in terms of another person's self-esteem, by listening carefully and asking thoughtful questions in order to understand them better. One of the most important qualities of a good communicator is his or her capacity for empathy, which is 'the ability to understand someone else's feelings as if they were one's own' (Collins English Dictionary). To achieve empathy, we must first be curious about how others are feeling and then encourage them to express themselves if they wish to.

How to talk:

Speaking in terms of our self-esteem means explaining to someone else where our emotions are really coming from, such as 'I feel (an emotion) because . . .'. It might take time for us to know how our self-esteem has been affected and, thus, to know what has generated our emotions, so sometimes we have to think carefully about why we feel as we do before communication can be most effective.

Saying 'I feel (negative emotion)', rather than 'you are making me feel (negative emotion)', is preferable because 'you are making me feel (negative emotion)' is likely to make the other person feel criticised and inclined to defend themselves. No one can make us feel anything we don't consent to, so we must first acknowledge that our feelings are our own, and they are not created by somebody else. It is unrealistic to think that we can avoid unpleasant emotions like anger, hurt, stress, and anxiety, but once we can understand that these emotions come from damage to our self-esteem, we can improve our ability to explain these emotions, rather than simply expressing them in their raw form or blaming other people for them. We may also then be able to reduce the potential our raw emotions have to cause harm via our subsequent behaviour to ourselves or others.

When we are expressing our thoughts and opinions, we should make particular effort not to appear to criticise the other person. Try to avoid words like 'You should . . .' or 'You ought to . . .' because these words give the impression that your opinion is more valid than the other persons, they imply criticism. If another person is accustomed to criticism from you or others, he or she may hear criticism no matter what you say or how you say it. In this case, try to be clear that you are expressing your feelings and opinions and why you have those feelings and opinions but that you want to hear the other person's as well because his or her feelings are just as valid and important. This is what people mean when they talk about not being afraid to 'set your own boundaries', that is, to express what negatively affects your self-esteem and why. This is also what is meant by being assertive (stating your own opinion), rather than aggressive (saying that someone else should feel the same).

How to listen:

Listening well is much harder than talking. We find it easy to see things from our own perspective, but really trying to understand someone else's perspective takes effort and patience. If we have a difficult relationship with someone and want to improve it, one of the best things we can do is to ask them thoughtful, open questions and listen carefully to the answers.

Open questions begin with what, where, how, why and when.

They are called open questions because they cannot be answered with yes or no. A closed question like 'Are you okay?' can be answered 'yes' or 'no' without providing much information. An open question like 'How are you feeling?' may encourage the other person to communicate more openly so we can begin to understand his or her feelings.

Of course, we have to want to understand the other person's point of view, which means forgetting about ourselves while we listen and making sure that we ask for clarifications about what he or she means in order to avoid misunderstanding. We all have habits that prevent us from listening well most of the time. We might be half-listening while we think about or do something else. We might 'switch off', particularly if the subject is highly emotional or potentially painful for us and we don't really want to hear the full details. We might interrupt before the person has finished, especially if we are afraid of hearing something we don't want to hear. We might try to mind-read and interpret for ourselves what the person means, rather than checking with them to be sure our assumptions are valid. We might listen selectively and hear only the parts of the other person's comments that support our point or fit our opinion. We might block the other person by laughing, crying, criticising, or doing something else that stops the conversation we are finding it difficult to have. There are many ways not to listen!

True communication involves listening more than talking. We have to want to understand others if we are going to become good communicators, and we have to be willing to try to explain ourselves as clearly as we can without blaming others for how we feel.

Arguments

Arguments are the opposite of good communication because we are usually so focused on defending ourselves and 'winning' that we are barely listening to the other person's point of view. When we have a major disagreement with someone and feel intense emotions about that issue, the threat to our emotional well-being causes us to experience the fight-or-flight response. The intense physical sensations during an argument occur because our nervous systems are mobilised by our brains' interpretation of the threat. We might feel our hearts racing or feel sweaty, agitated, or sick. In this overwhelming emotional state, it is difficult to think rationally about the situation, so our instinctive response is likely to be to defend our self-esteem by walking away, or attacking.

Arguments involve two people who are experiencing low self-esteem, because arguments centre on defending ourselves and/or criticising someone else. Arguments cannot occur unless both people participate; but while it takes two people to have an argument, it takes only one person to stop it.

If we are behaving like adults with good self-esteem, then we can disagree with someone without feeling hurt or taking things to heart because we will be able to explain ourselves clearly and accept that someone else might have a different opinion. If we are careful not to criticise the other person's opinion, but try instead to understand it, then the other person may be less likely to feel the need for self-defence, and an argument is less likely to happen. Any two people can easily become locked in cycles of bitter arguments that start off being about 'nothing'.

Sally

I had a bad day at work yesterday and came home hoping for some comfort from my partner, Gareth. He was busy with his own stuff though, and I became irritated that he didn't seem interested in listening to me. I didn't explain how I was feeling; I just got annoyed at him and criticised him for being selfish. He defended himself and argued back, calling me selfish. We ended up having a horrendous argument about 'nothing'. When we finally ran out of steam, we had a proper conversation about what had happened to me at work that day. I wish I had done that in the first place; criticising him was an unhelpful way to try to feel better. From now on, I will try to have the confidence to tell Gareth what is really going on for me, and I will try to listen to what is going on for him.

Apologising

How easy do we find it to apologise? Some people apologise all the time for minor accidents or mistakes, whereas others will never apologise because it makes them feel weak. Giving an honest apology is a clear sign of strength and good self-esteem because we are showing that we have the confidence to admit when we make mistakes and are not perfect.

After the intensity of emotion has passed, we can look at how the perceived threat to our self-worth, self-respect, or self-confidence caused the extreme emotions we were feeling at the time. After we have acknowledged where these emotions came from, we have the chance to understand them and take responsibility for them. Then we have a choice to apologise for our part in the disagreement, or not. While arguments can happen only if both sides participate, it can take a great deal of courage and self-confidence to look at our emotional reactions and explain and apologise for our behaviour, especially if we find it difficult to approach the person to whom we feel we should apologise.

By far the easier course is to stick fiercely to our point of view and refuse to apologise, but this approach shows that we don't have the strength to look at why we felt as we did and to explain our reaction. If we have good self-esteem, then we are able to take full responsibility for our emotions and actions and can acknowledge and apologise for our negative behaviour toward other people. We don't need always to be 'right' because we can acknowledge the value of other people's opinions, accept our own imperfections, and feel 'good enough', rather than hiding or defending our weaknesses and trying to appear perfect.

Battle of the Sexes

The 'battle of the sexes' is simply the tendency to attack each other's self-esteem based on our sex in order to feel better about ourselves. It is an ancient battle that millions of us still fight every day, particularly in our close relationships, at work, and in groups.

Men and women are equal, but they differ in important ways. We are different biologically, we have evolved differently over time, and we have different strengths and attributes, as well as many similar ones. We can complement each other well and can achieve far more together if we embrace each other's talents and abilities, however, we often feel threatened by the differences between us and argue with each other to prove our 'superiority'.

Historically, each sex has usually had its own clearly defined role. The value placed on these roles depends on the culture in which we live, but history has frequently seemed to place a higher value on the man's role than the woman's. There have also been imbalances between the sexes, such as women's voting rights, equal pay, and equal employment opportunities, and imbalances remain today. Therefore, it is no surprise that more women than men might suffer from feelings of low self-worth, self-respect or self-confidence. Most women are well aware that past generations (and some current cultures) often valued male babies over female babies, and that abuse of women in many different ways, was (and unfortunately still can be) commonplace. It is a fact that most men have greater physical strength than most women, so women in general know that they could be physically attacked or threatened by men, which can affect their self-confidence, self-worth or self-respect.

> 'I do not wish [women] to have power over
> men, but over themselves.'
> —Mary Wollstonecraft

On the other hand, the stereotype that women can multitask better than men and can 'do it all on their own' nowadays, including having children, can result in men feeling worthless and unnecessary, and can result in women disregarding the role of men in the belief that they can and should, as women, be able to do it all on their own.

> 'I don't know why women want any of the
> things that men have when one of the things
> that women have is men.'
> —Coco Chanel

> 'Demands for equality for women are threats
> to men's self-esteem and sense of sexual turf.'
> —Alice S. Rossi

Is either sex 'happy' when in competition with the other? I wish men and women had enough self-esteem to stop this ancient battle that serves no purpose other than to belittle each other and cause disharmony. We are different but equal, and if we can accept ourselves as we are, then we can accept the opposite sex as it is and embrace our differences, rather than undervaluing, mocking, or ridiculing them.

'It is a general mistake to think the men (or
women) we like are good for everything, and
those we do not, good for nothing.'
—Marquess of Halifax

How do you view the role you play as a man or a woman in your personal or working relationships? What do you expect from a male colleague, friend, or relative, in comparison to what you expect from a female colleague, friend, or relative? Do you agree with the stereotypes that pervade our society, or have you chosen for yourself the roles you are happy with in your relationships? Does the male/female battle play itself out in your relationships every day, or do you accept and value other people as individuals, regardless of their sex, or sexual orientation?

Happy Relationships

Michelle

I am the younger of two sisters, and we have an older brother. My parents travelled a lot when I was growing-up because of my father's job. My mother became pregnant young. I think she resented the travelling and being stuck at home with the children. They divorced when I was eight and my father has remarried twice since then and my mother once. Until I was seventeen, I lived on and off with both parents and their new spouses. I didn't feel wanted, no matter who I was with, and I didn't feel I belonged anywhere. I was a foreigner in foreign countries and a foreigner in my own country. My mother blamed me for not fitting in at each new school because I didn't try hard enough. I learnt quickly to try to change myself depending on the circumstances I was in, in order to be liked, but I never felt I really 'got it right' and I was certainly never 'myself' because I didn't know what that was.

By seventeen, I was sick of living under either of my parents' roofs, and I moved to a large city. I got a degree, but I will always be a failure in the eyes of my mother because of my unconventional lifestyle. My brother and sister are married with children; I don't know if they are truly happy, but at least they are fulfilling my mother's expectations. I got married in my early twenties, and quite soon afterwards, my husband became physically and psychologically abusive. I blamed his behaviour on myself and did everything I could to please him, but he always found something to be upset with me about, and he tried to control everything I did.

Eventually, with the help of close friends, I realised how abusive he was and found the courage to leave the marriage and to face being alone. I also had to face the disappointment and disapproval of my family, particularly my mother. After this, I had several brief relationships, and each time I tried to adapt myself to fit the other person so he would love me. But each time I wasn't able to keep it up, so the relationships ended with my feeling more unloved than I did before.

I married for the second time when I was thirty-four, and we have a daughter whom I adore. I suffered badly from post-natal depression though, and I began to drink heavily. My husband blamed me for not coping better and was not able to give me the support I needed. I blamed and criticised him, and he blamed and criticised me. We could not be supports to each other because we both needed more support and love than we could give.

I went for counselling after my husband requested a divorce. I felt desperately unhappy and stuck. I didn't want to be without him, I didn't want to put my child through a divorce like I had gone through as a child, and I didn't want another failed marriage. I wanted my husband to love me so I would feel okay, but after he asked for a divorce, I tried to improve myself and stopped drinking, but he still rejected me and he wouldn't come for counselling. I felt worthless, and being criticised yet again by my mother for 'screwing my life up' didn't help.

Gradually, through counselling, I have begun to look at my deeply rooted feelings of low self-worth and the lack of confidence I have in being who I am. I have always felt that I am not acceptable 'just as I am' because the people in my early life always wanted me to be how they thought I should be. I see now that I have always tried to please others so they would love me, but it hasn't worked because I have never known or loved myself.

I am trying to learn now what 'being myself' means, I think it will take me a while to sort out what I really believe and value from what I have let others tell me I should believe, do, or value. My relationships with men have all been about trying to be like them so they would like and love me; I haven't been able to choose partners who might really love me for myself because I wasn't being myself.

I have come to realise that my husband is not the right person for me, as we are too different and cause each other too much pain. I am worried for our daughter, but I hope that we can continue to love and provide for her separately, rather than together, as she means the world to both of us. I am desperate not to pass my own issues onto my daughter, so I am taking the time to nurture and get to know myself so I can be a happy and loving mother. If I can find a happy, healthy, and positive future for myself, then I know I can give my daughter the love and acceptance she needs, even though her father and I will not be together.

I am learning to accept my emotions and not to criticise them, but I am also looking at where they come from and how they are generated by my on-going feelings of low self-esteem. I will always carry deep-rooted feelings of criticism, mainly from my mother, but I am going to try to forgive her for this and to ask her to love me just as I am in the future, without criticism for the choices I make or have made in the past. This will be a difficult thing to ask, and she will probably feel criticised and defend herself because I realise now that her self-esteem is very low, too. She needs love and acceptance from me, so I am going to try to give her this, as well as asking for it in return.

I hope to find a life-long partner one day—someone with whom I can truly be myself and who loves me just as I am. There must be someone out there for me!

A happy relationship is one in which each partner has good self-esteem, and each helps the other to maintain that self-esteem, rather than criticising, insulting, or belittling each other in order to make themselves feel better. Your partner can be your closest friend and ally, but if you don't feel like this about him or her any longer, I hope this chapter can help you to improve your relationship.

'The more I travelled the more I realized that fear makes strangers of people who should be friends.'
—Shirley MacLaine

True love is an intense feeling of self-esteem because we feel we are being fully accepted by another person. Songs, poems, and books talk about love more than anything else because we all desire the blissful state of being loved by someone else just for who we are and loving them for who he or she is.

'Ultimately, love is self-approval.'
—Sondra Ray

The despair or frustration of lost or unrequited love can be one of the harshest pains we experience. If we picture our happiest moments in life, they are usually moments when we felt most loved.

The problem is that those we love and trust the most have the greatest potential to affect our self-esteem because we have become close to them and feel better about ourselves because they love us. If they appear to stop loving us, we can have difficulty thinking we are still good enough as people. Alexandra Stoddard's book, *Living Beautifully Together*, provides some explanations of how happy relationships work:

> 'The key to a successful relationship is
> self-esteem.'
> 'Each partner treats the other with kindness,
> tenderness, and love. That is the secret. If this
> seems overly simple, it is the truth.'
> 'Relationships aren't automatic, they require
> conscious attention. If we accept that all of
> us have difficulty understanding the inner
> life of the people to whom we are closest
> it helps us not to get upset when there
> are misunderstandings. Tolerance requires
> absolute honesty about our deepest feelings.'
> 'You can change yourself but you can't change
> others.'

We can change ourselves by taking charge of our self-esteem, and once we feel better about ourselves, we can hope to increase our partners' self-esteem by not needing to criticise them in order to feel better about ourselves. Then we can hope that they will change their critical behaviour toward us because they feel better about themselves and better about us. Again, Alexandra Stoddard explains how this approach works in marriage:

'The common thread in good marriages is the
loving, caring ways they treat each other. They
build each other up and are proud of their
partner.'
'Live as lovers. Lovers make a constant effort
to see that the needs of the other are met.
Lovers think of the other person's pleasure and
happiness.'

If you don't feel this way about your partner, you are not alone, as it is difficult not to let 'familiarity breed contempt'. The divorce rate is so high that being happily married sometimes seems unrealistic, but it is possible. However, whilst a loving relationship is what most of us want and value the most, films and fairy-tales portray 'happily ever after' as being instant and without effort, so we aren't shown what to do if the 'happiness' in our relationships begins to fade.

'The grass is always greener where you water it'
—Anonymous

Finding your 'happily ever after'.

Think back to the beginning of your relationship. Hopefully you will have chosen your partner in the first place because you both felt good self-esteem when you were in each other's company. What did you like about your partner when you were first getting to know him or her? Why did this make you feel good about yourself? What did you like to do together? What has changed now that makes you feel negative about your partner? Do you have unrealistic expectations now, where you used to think your partner was good enough just as he or she was? Not feeling good enough and not being loved for who we are feels terrible; the kindest thing we can do for someone else is to accept and love that person just as he or she is, without expecting him or her to be 'better' or different. If you can do this for your partner, just as you did at the beginning of your relationship, then you might be able to find happiness with each other again. If you can love unconditionally, he or she may stop feeling self-critical and critical of you and be able to love you unconditionally again as well. Somebody has to take the first step and stop the criticism. Will it be you?

Once you have stopped criticising your partner and yourself, take another look at your 'self-esteem pie'. Can you both accept what you cannot control, but change what you can? What activities could you be doing to help your self-esteem? What could you do together? What could you help your partner to do on his or her own that might improve his or her self-esteem? Once you stop the negative cycle and focus on reversing it, your relationship can go up and up and up!

Important: Relationship counselling is available to help you and your partner work through complex relationship issues, such as when a relationship is violent or abusive. If your partner is violent, abusive, or controlling and blames their actions on your 'making me do it', rather than taking responsibility for his or her own actions, then the relationship has an abusive element, and the person is unlikely to change without asking for professional help. In this situation, it is best to seek professional support, particularly if you are thinking of leaving the relationship and fear the consequences of doing so.

LOVE IS NOT ABUSIVE

'People will forget what you said, people will
forget what you did, but people will never
forget how you made them feel.'
—Maya Angelou

Low self-esteem has been used to justify the control or abuse of others, whether verbally, physically, sexually, financially or by any other means. A person might think they 'need' to behave abusively towards another person in order to feel stronger or better about themselves. Controlling or deliberately hurting others, especially those we perceive as weaker that ourselves, in order to feel 'stronger' or 'better' is never justified.

There are many forms of abuse in our society, and it is more widespread than we would ever want to believe. Millions of us experience or commit abuse every day. Most prevalent is the abuse of women by male partners, abuse of children by their parents or other adults, abuse of subordinates by those in power' in whatever capacity, and abuse of the elderly, the disabled, animals. Abuse is usually hidden from sight because abusers don't want to change what they are doing, they feel powerful. The abuser will justify their behaviour to themselves, and possibly to their victim(s). Those they are abusing might not recognise that they are being abused, or they might be powerless to avoid it or stop it.

We might all have times when we could be over-controlling those under our care or influence—those we might say we care about or love. We might be inflicting some or all of the following abuse to another person (or people), whether adult or child:

We have power and control over them and feel entitled to control them. We make them afraid of us by verbal insults and threats, belittling, undermining, manipulating, or humiliating them or using physical threats or punishments. We make excuses that 'it's because we love them' or 'because we want the best for them'. We believe we, not they, decide what is best for them. We disregard how they experience our behaviour and tell them how they should feel about us, themselves, and the other people in their lives. We think ourselves superior to them and manipulate those around us into agreeing with us that we are 'right'. We feel our control and power are justified and blame our victim or something or someone else for making us behave as we do. We minimise or deny our controlling behaviour. We strive to have a good public image to convince ourselves up that we are 'good' people and are justified in our control and power over someone else. We are possessive and think that the relationships we have with our victims means that we own them. (Details from Lundy Bancroft's *Why does he do that? Inside the minds of angry and controlling men*.)

Society, the victim, and those around the abuser can unconsciously accept and justify controlling behaviour by 'buying into' some or all of the several excuses for abuse, including that the abuser was abused, criticised, or neglected as a child or was hurt by someone else and the abuser hurts only people he or she loves so he or she 'can't help it'; the abuser finds it difficult to express feelings, so he or she explodes and lashes out; the abuser has a violent, angry, and aggressive personality that causes him or her to lose control and 'just go crazy'.

All of these descriptors and more might be true about a person who controls or hurts others, but they could equally be true about someone who chooses not to abuse others, but who instead takes responsibility for their negative behaviour and wants to change it.

Respect and abuse are opposites.

Manipulation and control of others is not justifiable; if we think that it is, then we will not recognise the abuse we might be committing, or which might be happening to us, or to someone close to us.

> 'Child abuse is still sanctioned—indeed, held
> in high regard—in our society as long as it is
> defined as child-rearing.'
> —Dr Alice Miller

If you think you or someone you know is being abused, seek professional help. A search online will bring up many sources of help.

Love

Mike

The thing I have realised about love is that what matters is whether a person actually feels loved or not. We might know we love someone, but if they don't feel it, then it is almost pointless as far as they are concerned.

I am an ex-abuser. I don't remember feeling loved as a child, so it has taken me time to work out what showing and receiving love means. For a long time I thought that showing love meant just saying I loved someone, or not even that: I thought that love was something people could assume for themselves. I didn't think I actually had to put effort into making sure people knew I loved them; I thought they should just know, regardless of my behaviour.

I used to hit my girlfriend. I was crazy about her from the moment we met, but I realise now that unconsciously I didn't feel I was good enough for her. I felt jealous if anyone else looked at her, and I blamed her if people flirted with her, even though it wasn't her fault. I started to control when she went out and who with, and I hated it if she was out without me or if she came home later than she said she would. I would go into a rage, and usually—especially if I was drunk—I ended up hitting her. But I would blame her for my behaviour because she had been the one who had missed the bus, or I would blame the football team I support for losing and making me feel angry. I told her I was jealous and became violent because I loved her so much. I told her I would kill her if she left me, because I needed her. I never stopped to think how she felt at all. I thought I was justified in controlling and abusing her because I needed to feel in control; I needed to stop her from leaving me so I had what I needed and would feel okay about myself.

I started to behave in a similar way toward my children from a previous relationship, and my ex-partner got a court order against me. At first, I blamed her for being unreasonable, but eventually I wanted to see my kids again, so I got some help.

At last I see that if a person we say we love doesn't feel the love we think we are showing them, then they are not receiving feelings of love and acceptance, and they will not benefit from our love for them. If we say we love someone, then it is our responsibility to show it to them in a way that means something to them.

I am still with my girlfriend, and we are getting married soon. I can't believe she has given me a second chance and I am determined to show that I deserve it, I am not going to let her down. She deserves all the love I can show her and more. I have asked her how she feels loved by me, and she says that she feels most loved and cared for when I cuddle her and do special little things for her like making her a cup of tea or rubbing her shoulders, or taking the bins out. She never trusted me saying 'I love you', because I always used to say that, even though I was abusing her. She would feel I was just saying it because it was easy to say and I didn't show I meant it.

I have a different way of feeling loved. I like kisses and cuddles, but most of all I like my girlfriend to say she loves me because hearing it makes it more real for me. I also like it when she buys little things for me—I don't mean a lot, but if she brings home something like my favourite chocolate bar, then I know she has been thinking of me and loves me, I never got even small presents when I was a child. It is the little things that mean the most, really. I realise though that I also have to believe that I am worthy of being loved (because I never felt loved as a child), so if my girlfriend has a hard day at work and doesn't remember to say she loves me, I don't panic anymore and assume the worst and think she doesn't love me anymore. I just trust that she does love me, and I focus on loving her that bit more at that time because she needs me to be there for her.

I have also started to think about when my kids might feel loved the most. One of them is very touchy-feely so I wrestle with him and hug him and tell him I love him loads. My little girl doesn't want hugs as much, but she loves it when we play a game together or make something, just the two of us. They are great kids, and because they know I love them now, we have a much better time together. They still want me to get back together with their mum, I think, but I hope they understand that we didn't split up because of them. I want them to know that I think they are great and that I will always be around for them when they need me, or even if they don't. (For more information on 'love languages' go to www.5lovelanguages. com or read Gary Chapman's *The Five Love Languages*.)

Whom do you love? Are you sure they know it? Do you tell them or show them in as many different ways as you can think of? When and how do you feel most loved? Can you tell people close to you when you feel most loved by them so that they know what you like?

Family Relationships— Labels and Expectations

Richard

I don't get on well with my family. They disappoint me, and I don't seem to be able to be around them without becoming angry or upset. I have older brothers who have always made me feel inferior. My parents ignored me because I was the youngest. I got married when I was eighteen to get away from my parents, but I was divorced by twenty-three because her mother hated me, and we argued about her all the time and about the children. We had two children, but I don't see my son. We worked together for a while, but then he didn't want to come into the business as a partner. I was very disappointed, and he left and doesn't get in touch much now. My daughter gets married soon and wants me to give her away. How am I going to make a speech and see all my family again when I hate most of them or they hate me? I don't seem to understand people or be able to talk to them. I don't think I'm a bad person, but maybe it's me.

Family relationships involve a whole list of labels:

Husband	Wife	Ex-husband	Ex-wife
Father	Daughter	Cousin	Grandparent
Mother	Son	Sister-in-law	Step-mother
Sister	Mother-in-law	Brother-in-law	Step-father
Brother	Father-in-law	Nephew	Step-brother

Half-brother	Half-sister	Niece	Step-sister
Grandson	Grand-daughter	Uncle	Aunt

What expectations do we place on these labels? We all have labels placed on us in relation to different relatives—do we know how we are supposed to behave in their eyes?

Most family conflicts arise when the people in a family do not meet the expectations of other members of that family. 'She should do that; she's my wife!' 'He shouldn't behave like that. He's my brother!' 'How could she speak to me like that? She's my cousin!' 'Why did he do that? He's my brother-in-law!' 'My husband/wife/father/ mother/sister/ daughter/son/brother let me down.'

Labels are unhelpful in relationships because the 'real' person behind the label is often disregarded and judged only by whether they meet the expectations of the label of daughter, son, sister, mother, grandparent, and so on. We are all individuals with our individual reasons for behaving as we do, and we cannot possibly meet all the expectations placed on us by others. We have all been guilty of expecting things from people just because of their relationship to us, but they might be completely unaware of the expectations we have and that we feel they are not meeting them.

Richard, part two

I have changed a lot recently and have come to see my family as a collection of individuals with the potential to be my friends. I realise that my older brothers have been fighting their own battles with my parents, brothers, or themselves. Their treatment of me was probably an attempt to feel better about themselves, rather than to put me down. My parents did ignore me when I was young, but they were busy people, with lots of responsibilities, they were doing their best and focusing on what they considered to be most important at the time. My ex mother-in-law probably didn't actually hate me; she probably hated her husband, who had been having an affair, so she took it out on me to drive me away and get closer to her daughter again. I wish I hadn't taken my feelings about my mother-in-law out on my wife, as it drove us apart. I see now that my son just didn't want to join the family firm, he wasn't trying to insult me personally; I just took it as a sign that he didn't respect me or care about me enough.

I am going to show my family who I am for the first time at my daughter's wedding. I am going to stop feeling sorry for myself and be friendly and kind and ask everyone what they have been up to. They might find the change in me strange, they might even respond angrily towards me, but I don't mind because this is how I want to be now, myself. My family can hopefully become my friends if I stop judging them by my own expectations; I want to get to know who they really are and to have the confidence to be myself around them for the first time.

CHRISTMAS, WEDDINGS, AND OTHER FAMILY OCCASIONS

Any occasion that brings together people who don't normally spend much time with each other can be stressful because of the uncertainty of how those people will make us feel. When our expectation that everything must be 'perfect' is added to the mix, such as is often the case at Christmas, weddings, and other family occasions, then it is even more likely that there will be tension and even conflict. The expectation of a wonderful day, followed by disappointment when it doesn't go as well as we expected, can be a blow to our self-esteem and leave us feeling very low.

The only way to avoid such an outcome is to have realistic expectations of ourselves and the occasion. The most important aspect of the day is likely to be spending positive time together as a family, not whether the flowers or food is perfect, so accepting and valuing people as they are, including ourselves, should ideally be our main focus. The details of the day—food, decorations, what we are wearing, and so on—might be important to us in terms of our own self-esteem (i.e., showing our ability to 'get it right'), but allowing people to have a good time is also important, so we have to find a realistic balance so our own stress levels don't ruin our or other people's enjoyment of the occasion. If we have worked hard, and our efforts are criticised or are insufficiently appreciated, we might have to work to control our self-esteem and remember that our own opinion of how we have done matters more than someone else's. It is likely that many people will compliment us, and we must not focus more on a single negative comment than we do on all the positive comments. If we do, then we have only ourselves to blame if we feel negative rather than positive about how the occasion has gone.

Motherhood

Andrea

When Olivia was born, I felt excited and wonderful, but I also felt terrified that I wouldn't be a good enough mother. I ended up with an emergency C-section because she wasn't coming out, and I remember feeling a failure because I hadn't given birth naturally like other people manage to do. She didn't breast-feed very well, and this felt like it must be my fault because it is supposedly a natural thing to be able to do. During the first few weeks, I was trying to get her into a routine like the books mention, but when she didn't fit into the routine I felt frustrated and thought I must be doing something wrong. I felt happy with myself only if a day went like the book said it should, it feels stupid to say that now. At the time though I had suddenly landed in a world where I did not have control anymore, so it took me time to realise that you cannot have control over a child; you can only adapt to their needs as best you can.

It took me a long time to adjust to the change to my life. The huge responsibility was the most terrifying thing, but also my body was different and I felt exhausted and emotional a lot of the time; it was like the person I was before had been scattered to the winds, and I had to pick up the pieces and find a new way of being 'me'. I felt frustrated that my life had become all about the baby, rather than about the other things I used to do and enjoy. Then I would feel guilty about not feeling fulfilled by this wonderful baby my husband and I had created, and I felt selfish that I should want anything other than to be caring for our daughter.

Other people at the mother-and-baby groups seemed to be doing a lot better job than I was; they probably weren't, though. They seemed to be taking everything in their stride and constantly talked about all the wonderful and 'important' things they had done with their babies, or had bought for them. Looking back, I think I put too much energy into comparing myself to them, I worried about making her room nice, and buying her nice clothes and a fancy pram, and I didn't really stop to think about what she really needed from me. No book can teach you how to show love to your child, and with all the endless advice and information that is given to new mothers I think it can actually be easy to forget that love is the most important thing. I could have saved more of my energy and focused on accepting myself and simply loving Olivia, rather than spending so much time worrying about anything or anyone else. I don't think I had post-natal depression; I think these feelings are normal for new mothers to a greater or lesser extent. I am doing better now. I am accepting that I am not an 'earth-mother' type of person, I do still get frustrated with all the endless tasks of motherhood, but that's ok because I make sure I find time for things which I really enjoy, both with Olivia, and on my own.

Heather

I was having my first child. I felt excited about going into labour and having Thomas because I wanted to meet him. I was nervous, but I had no reason to think it would go badly; I thought I was prepared. Once labour started, however, I felt terrified and out of control. The midwives and my mother did their best, but the pain frightened me, and I didn't know if I could do what was expected of me.

The birth didn't go very well: I ended up with an epidural and forceps delivery and was very torn. Looking back, I think it was because I was so anxious and fearful. My mum thought she was being supportive, but she was making constant suggestions about what I should be doing, or saying how well she had done when she gave birth to me, which wasn't helpful to hear. I didn't feel confident or in control, so I don't think I was able to handle the birth in a very positive way.

Once Thomas came out, I didn't really feel anything except relieved; I didn't feel an immediate connection with him because it had been such a frightening and negative experience. I took him home and began the process of coping, and most of the time I didn't cope very well at all, I was constantly exhausted. Midwives and health visitors came, but I felt I had to conceal how I was really feeling or they might criticise me further and tell me I wasn't doing well enough as a mother. I ended up with severe post-natal depression, and it has taken me a long time to recover and feel good enough as a mother. I love Thomas more than anything, but I still have feelings of guilt that I felt so detached from him and myself for such a long time at the beginning of his life. I have to forgive myself for something I couldn't control, and be gentle with myself so that I can show myself and him all the love possible from now on.

Becoming a mother can be one of the most rollercoaster-like experiences in terms of our self-esteem. We often feel an increase in self-esteem when we become pregnant because, if it was a planned pregnancy, we are meeting the expectations of ourselves, our partners, our families, and society. If the pregnancy was not planned, however, then the news can be hard to take in because it means many things in terms of our self-esteem. Are we happy? Sad? Frightened? What if we don't want to be pregnant and decide to have an abortion?

Dawn

I had an abortion when I was seventeen. I didn't tell my parents because I knew they would be so disappointed and ashamed that I had got pregnant. I don't remember thinking of it as a baby—just as something that I had to make go away. I told my boyfriend at the time and, thankfully, he came with me. It was awful because it suddenly became real, and I realised what I was doing. I couldn't believe it was happening to me, but I didn't feel I had any choice but to get on with it.

I look back now, and I grieve for the baby I didn't have. Over the years I have cried about it and have felt angry at my parents for being so strict and judgmental that I felt I couldn't tell them I was pregnant. Maybe I would have had the child if I could have told them, maybe they would have loved him or her, but I didn't think that was likely at the time. I have blamed myself for being weak and scared of my parents' reaction, or the doctors and nurses for not getting me counselling before I made my decision. Ultimately, though, I have forgiven myself. It was a frightening and impossible situation to be in, and I did what I felt I had to do at the time. It was a horrible decision to have to make, and I feel endless sympathy for all the millions of women who have had to face a similar decision. My heart goes out to them, no matter what their situation, or what they decided to do.

If a pregnancy progresses, there can be mixed feeling in terms of self-esteem. We can feel wonderful to be creating a new life and find our changing shape attractive, or we can feel acutely the loss of our previous body shape and our freedom to live as we did before. The arrival of a baby is treated by society as a time of joy, but for the parents, particularly the mother, there can be a seesaw of emotion. The birth can give our self-esteem a wonderful boost, but it can also negatively affect it because of what may have changed, such as our freedom to consider only ourselves, our choices about work, having to rely on a partner for income and support, feeling exhausted and less desirable because of physical changes, and so on.

Fiona

I think, as mothers, we often don't stop to think about the huge upheavals we go through during pregnancy, childbirth, and the years afterwards. We are not gentle enough on ourselves. We pick up on expectations from somewhere that we should be superhuman and should be able to achieve and cope with more than is physically possible. I think most of us need to be gentler with ourselves and give ourselves adequate recognition for what we achieve, rather than criticising ourselves or taking ourselves for granted. Motherhood is a job with more challenges (and rewards) than probably any other, and we need to recognise these and make sure that we accept who we are and what we do without comparing ourselves to others, or expecting ourselves to achieve more or to 'be perfect'.

A fellow mother said to me, 'Everyone feels like a terrible mother at one time or another', and I think she is right. Our self-esteem as parents needs monitoring almost constantly because children change all the time and make new demands of us, or they have new questions and new feelings and emotions within themselves. If we can consistently 'keep calm' by maintaining our own feelings of self-worth and self-confidence, then we will be doing the best job we can to help our children with their own self-esteem. It is natural to feel like a failure or a bad parent sometimes, and we need to give ourselves a break when we feel negative, but if we can pick ourselves up and accept our imperfections, then we can hopefully bring up resilient and happy children who are positive about themselves and can handle their own negative feelings in a calm and accepting way.

'Before you drive a car, you need a
state-approved course of instruction, but
driving a car is nothing, nothing, compared to
living every day with a husband and raising up
a new human being.'
—Anne Tyler

Parenting

Sam

I am finding being a parent a privilege and an adventure, but there are times when it drives me crazy and I feel miserable. Sometimes the demands they make of me can feel too much, and I get really frustrated with them. They might fight, make a mess, break something, and demand my attention all at the same time, and I find myself hating those times because I feel overwhelmed and angry that they are so demanding. Afterward, I feel guilty and ungrateful for the wonderful children I have, and I worry they will feel unloved and negative about themselves because I have become frustrated and shouted at them. I have smacked them at times, too, and I always feel terrible afterwards because I wish I could have controlled my frustration and accepted that they are just young children and are not deliberately trying to annoy me.

For a long time, I felt that I didn't know how to be a good parent. Parenting felt like it was all about saying no and being cross. I imagined that other people's children did what they were told and respected their parents, but I didn't know how to make that happen. I felt disrespected and 'not good enough', which is what made me so mad.

It took me a long time to realise that I had to accept myself as 'good enough' and to stop thinking that I wasn't as good as other parents. I needed to look at the expectations I had of myself and my children and where those expectations came from. I believed my children should do as they were told just because

I demanded it and shouted at them, but this was having the opposite effect because it made them fearful and resentful and made them believe they were naughty children who didn't know how to behave. I wasn't letting them be themselves.

Now I am much kinder. I have decided that it is more important not to shout at them than it is to 'get things right'. If they don't want to get up in the morning, I now try to find a light-hearted way to get them downstairs, rather than being cross as I would have been before. I don't want to be that kind of parent anymore. I try to stick to observations, such as 'It seems someone is still in bed when it's time to get up', rather than being negative and cross and saying something like 'Get out of bed now or there's no treat later'. With things that used to be a battle, I now try to encourage them, rather than demanding and shouting at them. That doesn't mean I give in; in fact, it has become easier to set rules and standards because I feel more calm and confident now, so I know I am being fair and consistent in what I ask of them. I used to insist on things 'because I said so', and I wouldn't always say please to them. Now, though, I am always polite, so I am teaching them to be polite, and the things I insist on are only the ones that I think really matter.

I can't believe how I have changed, and I am so much happier because of it. I still get annoyed or frustrated sometimes when I am tired or particularly stressed—I don't expect to be perfect—but generally speaking, I listen now to why my children don't want to do things, and I explain why I want them to. We aim for 'win-win' solutions, rather than 'lose-lose' solutions, and all try to help each other and make life more fun. I try to show my children the kindness, courtesy, and respect that I would like them to show to me. I have the confidence now to apologise to them when I have forgotten something or made a mistake, rather than defending myself and trying to appear perfect or always in control. I recently heard them saying 'sorry' to each other spontaneously, which I never thought would happen!

Because I am being less demanding of my children and being more realistic about my expectations, I am enjoying being a parent more, and I am taking more interest in building our collective self-esteem as a family. I am trying a policy of not being cross as long as they tell me the truth, even if they are admitting to doing something wrong. I try to understand why they might have thought what they did was right for them at the time, rather than criticising them for it. I want them to feel that they are good people who might occasionally do bad or silly things, rather than that they are 'bad children'. I hope that, as they grow up, they will feel that they can tell me even things they are ashamed of, rather than lying for fear of disapproval or punishment (which is how I behaved with my own parents), and that they know they will get a loving and understanding response.

Being a partner and a parent whilst working and fitting in all the other parts of life is still pretty exhausting, but now I am not feeling so frustrated with myself and everyone else. I used to see life as an endless list of jobs to do and hurdles to jump before I could 'be happy', but it's not like that anymore. I am accepting that life has its hard parts, and there is no point fighting them. I need to accept them and find joy in them somewhere. The house is messier now because I am less of a perfectionist, but the people in it are happier, which is much more important!

Parenting is surely the hardest job in the world? There is no training, no qualification, no exam to pass; for the most part, we have to figure out how to be parents on our own. Being a parent presents many opportunities to feel good about ourselves and to experience improved self-worth, self-respect and self-confidence—and as many, if not more, opportunities to feel out of control and to experience feelings of low self-esteem.

Do we want to be leaders or bullies? We sometimes feel a need to control and 'win' with our children, no matter what, so we feel in control. However, in giving in to this need we are likely to be taking self-esteem away from our children and causing them insecurity, which they might take out on themselves or others. The most important thing we can do for our children is to love them unconditionally and tell them that they are good enough, rather than criticising them. We all flourish if we believe in ourselves and don't feel criticised. Happy children are loved and respected, so they can show love and respect to others. They are not forced to respect, because true love and respect cannot be forced.

> 'Too often, I think, children are required to write before they have anything to say. Teach them to think and read and talk without self-repression, and they will write because they cannot help it.'
> —Anne Sullivan

If we find being a parent challenging and miserable at times, we can stop and acknowledge those feelings. Rather than blaming ourselves, we can take time to look at how we can accept ourselves as being 'good enough', rather than comparing ourselves to others, being self-critical, and lowering our own self-esteem. We can think about the kind of parents we would like to be, and if we have partners, we can aim to raise their self-esteem by supporting, not criticising, them. However, we can also be honest with them about how we feel and about how we would like their understanding and support. Then, together, we can be a better and happier parenting team. If we show more love and gentleness to ourselves, we can be more loving and accepting toward our partners and children, and if that is all any of us achieve on a particular day, then I think that is plenty.

Emma

I am a single parent. I hear comments in the media about absent fathers and single-parent families being one of society's greatest issues, and I feel insulted. It is sad that so many relationships fail, but those of us who cope by ourselves and still manage to bring up pleasant well-behaved children should be hugely admired. I agree that 'fatherless-ness' is widespread, and I think that the main reason it causes so many problems is that children without effective fathers can easily feel unwanted or abandoned by them, and can begin to question their own self-worth at a very deep level. This can affect their self-confidence and ability to thrive.

My father left when I was five, and I know that children who have an absent parent often believe the parent is not there because the children are somehow not worthy of being loved by that parent and were not worth staying around for, even though this is usually not the case. A single parent with good self-esteem is just as capable as two parents of bringing up a loving and positive child, especially if that single parent also continues to have a positive relationship with his or her ex-partner or with other family members so the child has additional role models and sources of love and support. A married couple who stay together just for their children's sake but who fight all the time, belittle and undermine each other, and use their children as emotional pawns between them, are not showing signs of good self-esteem and are more likely to damage rather than foster the self-esteem of their children. I think this is just as much of a problem in society as single parenting might be.

'How sad that man would base an entire
civilization on the principle of paternity, upon
legal ownership and presumed responsibility
for children, and then never really get to know
their sons and daughters very well.'
—Phyllis Chesler

'If survival depended solely on the triumph of
the strong, then the species would perish. So
the real reason for survival, the principle factor
in the 'struggle of existence', is the love of
adults for their young.'
—Maria Montessori

Jodie & Duncan—Sibling Rivalry

We have two sons who fight all the time. The older one picks on his younger brother a lot, and what worries us most is that he is starting to become a bully at school. We have tried everything—physical punishments, bribery, banning video games, grounding—but nothing seems to work. We have started arguing more about it with each other, too, which isn't helping.

We talked things through with his teacher and headmaster and thought about a different way to approach things. We realised that our son's behaviour was likely to be about wanting our attention; he was just getting it through doing negative things, rather than positive things. We also began to wonder whether our older son might think the younger one was loved more than he was and whether we really loved him at all because we shout at him so much. Our older son was starting to believe he was a bad boy because we were treating him like one, so he continued to behave as we expected him to—badly. He was beginning to want to feel better about himself by being powerful over 'weaker' children in school.

Something had to change. Firstly, we worked on our partnership and stopped criticising each other, instead accepting that we both wanted the same thing, so we supported and encouraged each other. After this, we both concentrated on the boys and thought about how to let them know that they were loved just for who they are. We hugged them more, told them we loved them, rewarded them with time for special activities, and so on. We also stopped reacting negatively to negative behaviour and instead saw that competition for love and attention was behind their behaviour. We talked about this by saying that we loved them both and that they could be good brothers who didn't need to criticise and pick on each other to feel more important and better about themselves.

It was a hard time, but we quickly felt we were getting somewhere with our calm and loving approach. Gradually, the boys changed their thoughts about themselves and started to mimic our positive behaviour. They are now happy boys who generally play well together and love and support each other most of the time! They know they are loved by us, and we are a happy family at last.

There are many books and websites on positive parenting, www.positiveparenting.com, www.parenting.org.uk, www.goldfishsmiles.com are ones I have come across.

Affairs

Graham

We have been married for almost ten years. Our relationship was initially strong, but after a few years our sex life dwindled for a variety of reasons. We had young children, we were always tired with not much time to ourselves, and Alison found sex painful at times, so I didn't want to pressure her. We still remained an affectionate couple, and I felt proud that I wasn't hung up on needing sex, but I see now that under the surface our relationship began to stagnate and suffer. We were becoming friends occupying the same house, rather than being a close intimate husband and wife team like we had started out being. We just ignored this and got on with things though because I don't think we knew how to make things better, and we didn't want to upset each other. As a man, I felt unable to talk about things very well having never had any practice talking about emotional issues, so ignoring my feelings was the easier option.

We went to counselling after Alison found out about an affair I had with a woman I met through work. I felt embarrassed and mortified going for counselling because I couldn't explain my stupid and appalling behaviour. I didn't love the person I had an affair with, and I desperately didn't want to lose Alison. I wanted her to believe me and to forgive me, but I didn't know if I could ever forgive myself. I wanted to understand why I had done it and to feel confident that I really wouldn't do anything so stupid again. I wanted to earn Alison's trust again and to convince her that she could trust me in the future.

Alison

I didn't know whether to go for counselling or not. I was devastated when I found out about the affair and all the lying that had gone with it, but I also knew that I loved my husband and loved the life I thought we had built together. I didn't know if I could leave and affect our children by taking them away from their father, and I didn't know if starting again would be the best option for me, but I also didn't want to be perceived by others and myself as a doormat who stayed with someone just because I had nowhere else to go. I felt betrayed, rejected, and humiliated, and I didn't know whether I should leave or stay. In the end I decided that we should look together at what must have gone wrong in our relationship. My main aim for counselling was to see whether we could both come to understand why Graham had the affair and whether I could ever forgive him and trust him again so we could rebuild our life together.

Graham

When we looked carefully at the impact our reduced sex life had on our relationship, we realised that it had had a much bigger effect than we knew at the time. I thought I was handling not having much sex really well, but as soon as it was handed to me on a plate by someone who showed interest in me, and with the additional confidence of alcohol, I took it. I still feel ashamed that I feel I had become a sad, middle-aged man with low self-esteem who needed to feel better about himself by having sex with a younger woman, and then tried to hide it from his wife. I had never considered my self-esteem before. I hadn't been able to explain even to myself why I risked my marriage for a woman I didn't care about.

We started to look at all the things that have always been good in our relationship, and there are many. We love each other and want to be an intimate team again, we recognise now that a fulfilling sexual relationship is a vital part of our relationship. Alison decided to seek medical help in order to hopefully resume a pain-free sex life. In the meantime, we know we need to reconnect with each other and we are finding time to rebuild trust and intimacy in lots of different ways.

Alison

I didn't know whether our marriage could be saved or whether I could ever understand why Graham did what he did, but now I do. I forgive him. Sometimes I joke that I wish I could have run off and had an affair as well to improve my self-esteem, but I am only joking. I have more confidence now in talking to the doctor about improving my sex life. We are now improving our self-esteem together by finding things we both enjoy, including rebuilding our sexual intimacy. It hasn't been easy, but I am glad that we both found the strength to look at our situation, to admit our mistakes, and to do something about them. If we hadn't done this, we would probably have got divorced without ever understanding why it all went wrong, and the rest of our lives might have been negatively affected as a result.

Before we choose to have an affair, whatever the reason, we are experiencing a period of low self-esteem. We usually know that an affair is probably not a good idea but we don't know how to fix our current relationship so if an opportunity to have an affair is presented, we may take it to feel better about ourselves. Being wanted by someone else, especially secretly, can give a great boost to our self-esteem.

Sometimes people who have an affair will tell their partners. Perhaps they cannot live with the guilt, and their self-esteem tells them that they have to tell their partners because they don't like who they have become or because they have decided to leave the relationship. Once the affair is disclosed or discovered, it usually has an impact on the self-esteem of both partners. The person who had the affair often feels even worse about himself or herself than ever, and the partner who was cheated on often feels betrayed and not good enough to be faithful to. Most people eventually regret an affair even if it is not discovered, because what they usually wanted in the first place was to be happy in their original relationship, but they don't know how to achieve that, so they take an easier decision and start a relationship with someone else. The temporary improvement in self-esteem that they feel by having an affair usually, ultimately, makes everything worse.

The partner who is wronged might feel a big drop in self-esteem; an affair can feel extremely humiliating, embarrassing, and hurtful. It is difficult to forgive an affair because our self-esteem is likely to be significantly affected by the betrayal of someone we love and trust. In order to forgive and see the good in our partner again, we need to be able to take control of our own self-esteem and decide that we are okay, regardless of what our partner chooses to do. Affairs do not occur because the wronged partner is not good enough, but because of how the person who has the affair felt about himself or herself at the time they made that choice. Therefore, it is possible to feel okay about ourselves even if we have been cheated on because the other person's affair had to do with his or her desire to feel better, rather than with rejecting us. Even so, the revelation of an affair is not easy to deal with, because the other person has behaved selfishly and has breached their partners trust.

Wronged partners often need to look at their own self-esteem within their relationship before the affair happened. Often, they will also have been experiencing low self-esteem for some reason, so they may have been defending themselves and criticising their partner, or unconsciously contributing to their partner's low self-esteem in some way, which triggered their partners' decision to have an affair. This does not justify their partner's decision, but there is always a reason why an affair seems like a good idea at the time. I wish we were able to be more aware at the time of the long-term consequences of our decisions, because choosing to have an affair, perhaps under the influence of alcohol or sexual excitement can have more enduring consequences than virtually any other thing we might do.

Charlie & Tim

I had an affair last year when I fell in love with a colleague at work. We resisted sleeping together for as long as we could because we were both married, but the love we felt for one another was so strong that it was inevitable that we would end up in bed together eventually. When Tim found out it had been going on for six months, and I was ready to leave my marriage. Ben had already told his wife he was leaving.

I told Tim, and it was awful; he was more devastated that I expected and he insisted we go for counselling. I didn't want to because I knew how I felt and that nothing would change it, but out of respect for Tim I agreed to go, because I had been the unfaithful one, but also because I wanted him to see that our marriage was truly over. I hoped that after counselling he would let me move on.

In counselling we talked first about our upbringings, the ups and downs of our lives before we met, why were initially attracted to each other, and what had happened in our relationship since we had been together. I loved Tim from the moment I saw him. I am an only child and have always been quite shy. Tim was the most popular guy in our group of friends and part of me never felt quite good enough for him or felt that I really deserved him. When he said he loved me I was over the moon. I fell pregnant only a year after we got together, but he was delighted and proposed to me. Though I lost the baby, we still married, and it was the happiest day of my life. Our future seemed bright, despite our recent loss.

After that, it slowly seemed to go wrong. Tim was very busy at work, and I was trying to get my own career going despite still grieving for our lost baby. I think we still loved each other, but the day-to-day issues of life seemed to get in the way. Month by month, I failed to get pregnant, and we struggled to talk about it. Sex lost any spontaneity, and I think we both felt miserable. I started to feel more and more lonely, and I wondered whether Tim regretted marrying me after all. Perhaps I had just been a trophy wife; he had always commented on how attractive I look, but I wondered whether he had ever really loved me for who I am inside? When I met Ben, I knew it was different; I could be myself with him, and we spent hours talking about our lives. I felt happy and good about myself for the first time in ages.

I went for counselling with Tim once a week for eight weeks. I didn't think it could make any difference, but gradually I realised that I was hearing and saying things that Tim and I had never heard or said before. I heard how Tim had really felt about me when we met: he had admired much more about me than my looks, and he was shocked to discover that I had felt insecure about how he felt about me and whether I was good enough for him. We both talked about our grief at losing our baby and about how hard we had both found it not to be able to conceive again. It felt like I was seeing and hearing Tim for the first time in years. We had stopped communicating, and it took my affair to make us talk and listen to each other again.

The counselling confused me. I loved how I felt about myself when I was with Ben, but now I was remembering why I loved Tim so much and realising how much he had always loved me. How could I throw away the years we had spent together and everything we had been through? I knew I had to figure out who I loved and why. Tim had every right to hate me and blame me for wrecking our marriage, but he was being incredible to be giving me another chance. He said, if I really loved Ben, then he wouldn't stand in my way, but he believed we had something special that he was determined to fight for. He said he could forgive me if we could figure out what had gone wrong and could find a new and better relationship. Ben had left his wife and was waiting for me to finish with counselling so we could be together. How long would he wait for me to make a decision?

I had some counselling sessions on my own and admitted how confused and guilty I felt. We talked about my self-esteem and why I felt different about myself when I was with Tim than when I was with Ben. I had to figure out who I really was, what mattered to me, and what I really wanted in life. I realised that I had had serial relationships since I had been seventeen, and I didn't remember how it felt to be on my own. It was the first time I had really considered what made me, me. Once I looked carefully at myself, started to feel better about who I am, and thought about the type of partner who would be right for me, the answer became clear. I wanted someone who really knew himself, felt comfortable with who he is, and who really wanted to know me and to love me for who I am.

The counselling changed my life because for the first time I felt free to accept myself and felt sure about which person was right for me. I felt terribly guilty and upset about telling the other person that I had made my decision. It was the hardest thing I have ever had to do, and I desperately didn't want to hurt him, but I knew that I had to be honest. He deserved to be with someone who could truly love him, not with me for the wrong reasons.

Recovering from an affair

I think the process of moving on from an affair involves asking ourselves some or all of the following questions:

The one who was cheated on: How do I feel at the moment in terms of my self-esteem? Do I have the strength to decide for myself what I should do now? Will I feel stronger if I leave or if I stay? How will I be influenced by other people's opinions of the 'right' thing to do? Can I admit the part I played in our relationship's not being as good as it could have been? Can I look at my own self-esteem before the affair and my partners' and how we were influencing each other?

Can I be a person who understands why my partner had the affair? Can I forgive him or her because I love him or her, because nobody is perfect, and because he or she is asking for my forgiveness? Can I try again, or is it better for both of us if our relationship is over? Can I truly let the affair go and love and trust my partner again in such a way that it doesn't taint our relationship forever? Can I start again in the future with someone else? Can I choose to be on my own?

The one who cheated: How do I feel right now in terms of my self-esteem? How am I coping with the opinions and judgment of others? Can I figure out why I needed to improve my self-esteem by having an affair? Can I admit the reason I did it? If I want forgiveness from my partner, can I ask for it and cope with whatever his or her answer is? Can I forgive myself if I understand what lay behind my decision? Can I be honest about wanting to stay or wanting to leave? Can I ask for forgiveness from others? If I want to stay and try to be forgiven, can I wait until my partner feels he or she can forgive me? Can I accept his or her decision and get on with my life if he or she decides he or she can't?

Parents in an affair: Can we put aside our own hurt feelings when it comes to focusing on our children and what they need? Can we protect their self-esteem and allow them to keep as positive an image of their other parent as possible? If they hear criticism of either parent or feel rejected by a parent, they are likely to question their own self-worth, making their future even more difficult than it might otherwise be. How can our children know the truth eventually without feeling worse about themselves?

DIVORCE

Chris

I have just been through a horrendous divorce. We fought about the money, the kids, the furniture, the dog—everything. I can't believe we were ever happily married. We had an amazing wedding; it cost a fortune and everything was perfect, but looking back now, it feels like all we cared about was how everything looked and whether we had got everything right in the eyes of our friends. We weren't actually focusing on preparing to love each other unconditionally for the rest of our lives. We went from being crazy about each other to being strangers and then enemies in the same house. When the divorce process started, we just fought each other. I am so glad it is all over now, but I feel like I have been scarred for life and will never have a meaningful relationship with anyone ever again.

It has all been about loss. I have gained my freedom, but I have lost the marriage I hoped to have, my life partner, the status of being married, time with my children, money, our house, possessions, friends. I feel completely washed out by the whole process, and I barely know who I am at the moment. Sometimes I want to just stay in bed and hide, or I get drunk, or I have meaningless sex with strangers to feel better about myself. I feel very bitter toward my ex-spouse. What has he turned me into? How have I become like this? What can I do about it, or is this how I am going to feel from now on?

Six months later

My drinking was becoming more and more of a problem, and thankfully a friend convinced me to go to the doctor because my friend thought I was depressed. I ended up on antidepressants, and through the counselling I was offered, I began to look at my life and what it had become. I started off blaming everything on my ex. It wasn't my fault that we had argued so much, it wasn't my fault that the marriage went sour, it wasn't my fault that the kids stopped talking to me, etc. Everything was somebody else's fault, not mine.

Gradually, I changed my outlook. I saw that I had been living a life full of expectations, disagreements, and criticism of others. I had wanted my husband to behave a certain way, and when he didn't, I criticised him. I didn't show any interest in asking what he wanted or needed. I didn't love him as he was. I wanted my children to enjoy certain things and be a certain way and felt critical of them if they were different from how I thought they should be. No wonder they stopped talking to me!

And I was judgmental of myself. I thought being good enough meant putting everything I could into my work and achieving my full potential. I think I got this idea from my father, but I didn't realise until it was too late that this meant I was sacrificing the other areas of my life. When I did realise it, I blamed other people for the decisions I had made, rather than recognising that my self-esteem had been reliant on doing well at work and being successful in the eyes of others. I even fought my way through the divorce because I thought that giving in on anything would mean I was weak. What I see now is that a stronger person would have had the self-esteem to be fair and to admit her mistakes.

I am trying to live a different life now. I can see where I went wrong in my marriage, and I have apologised to my ex. It wasn't easy, and I don't think we will ever get back together, but at least things are better than they were. He wasn't perfect either, but I have forgiven him for some of the things he said and did to me because I can see now that he was defending and protecting himself. My relationship with my children is getting better. They are distrustful of me, and I can see that they expect criticism from me, rather than support, but I am trying to show them that I love them just as they are. I am doing even better at work now that I am not drinking and am less stressed. I am pleased about that, but I actually see work as less important than I did in terms of my self-esteem, so I am finding time for other things that bring me pleasure, and my life is richer as a result.

Maybe in the future I will find a partner I can truly love for who he is and who truly loves me. I don't think I want to get married again, but if I did, I would have a simple ceremony that meant what it was supposed to mean, rather than the showy, expensive, and ultimately meaningless one I had before. For now, though, I am happy by myself and am focusing on improving the relationships that are already in my life.

Bereavement

Nicola

I lost my mum last year to cancer. I am an only child, and we were very close. My dad went to pieces. I try to see him every day, but seeing him makes me feel worse, and I am finding it hard enough to cope with my own grief. I am married, and my husband is doing his best, but I think he is starting to feel frustrated with me. I feel like I should be able to get over this and be able to carry on with my life, but my grief is like a huge, dark hole that I can't climb out of. I have lost such a big part of my life that I don't think I will ever feel whole again, I don't feel able to cope without her.

I have been reading about the five stages of grief described by Elizabeth Kubler-Ross, and I see now that I definitely went through them when she was dying and am still experiencing some of them now. I was in denial about her illness for quite a long time, and dad never really came round to it until well after she was gone. I think that's why it hit him harder, because he didn't believe it would actually happen. I have been through periods of intense anger, and I can still feel angry sometimes that this has happened to me and to dad, and I can feel angry at myself for not being okay yet and with my husband and other people for not understanding. Anger is tiring, though, and I can't stay that way for long. I definitely went through bargaining, too. I used to pray to God for more time and promised that I would be a better person if she could live, and I am angry at God that my bargaining didn't work. Most of the time I guess I feel like I am in the depression stage; some days I can get on with life a bit, but other days the total exhaustion returns, and I don't seem to see the point in anything, and I feel totally alone and just cry. Apparently this means I am starting to accept the situation, so it is a good thing, but it doesn't feel good; it feels bleak and never-ending.

One of the hardest parts of grief is coping with the reactions of other people toward me. I remember not knowing what to say to a friend whose husband died, and now I am realising how much more lonely grief is because people don't know what to say. Most people just look at me sympathetically or avoid me. I don't blame them, but I want to say to them, 'Please just say or do something kind. It doesn't matter what, but if you can just make any kind gesture, then life won't seem so bleak and I won't feel so misunderstood and alone.' When someone is kind to me or asks how I am feeling, for that moment I smile and I know someone cares for me and that there might be a chink of hope. Maybe, gradually, if I can reach out to others, accept their kindness, and be kind in return, then those moments might turn into minutes—and then perhaps hours—away from the gaping hole of grief.

Acceptance is the final stage, but I don't know if or when I will get there, and I am telling myself that's okay. People grieve in different ways and at different speeds. I think the main thing I need to learn little by little is that I can be okay without my mum but that I can still draw comfort from her memory. For a while I felt that only having her back would make me feel okay, but now, at times when I would have spoken to her, I will feel okay that I can't because I realise I can cope on my own with whatever it is or with the help of my husband or friends. I will always miss her terribly, but perhaps I will be able to find greater strength within myself because I have been through this loss. I am determined to be there for my dad and to help

87

him to find his strength again. I hope he will, but I think that being there for him is helping me to be stronger and to accept that Mum has gone but will never be forgotten. I am realising, too, that life must be about the living. My husband is still here, and if I neglect him, then I am allowing my grief to colour everything in my life. My mother certainly wouldn't want that for me. She wouldn't want me to feel sorry for myself and to be consumed by grief. She would want me to laugh and love and live, so that is what I am going to try to do more and more from this day on. I frequently read the poem, 'Do Not Stand at my Grave and Weep' by Mary Frye, and it makes me feel better.

WORK

Peter

I hate my job. My boss is a bully, and all I get is criticism and blame if things go wrong and no thanks or credit if things go well. I am miserable and feel like I am bad at my job, but I have nowhere else to go. I am bored and resentful now, so I know I am working less hard and am starting to deserve the criticism I am getting, but I don't like or respect my boss, so I don't want to do things just because she says I should. She's just interested in pleasing the bosses above her, rather than listening to me. Whatever I do is wrong anyway, so what's the point?

I went to one of these team-building 'motivational' days, and it helped to change my perspective. The leader asked how much we valued what we do for a living and whether, if we could value ourselves and what we do more, we might do a better job and consequently feel better about ourselves. If we were doing a better job, we might get more recognition, which would help to further increase our self-esteem.

One of the sessions was on personal appearance and whether we always dressed in a way that helped us to feel good about ourselves at work. Apparently, taking care of our appearance at work has been found to have a significant motivational effect on the individual and their colleagues because it shows that we each respect ourselves, our job, and those we work with.

We also looked at our behaviour at work. Whatever position we were in, we had to look at whether we criticised our colleagues, employees, or boss in order to feel better about ourselves. Did we show good self-esteem in our ability to be fair and consistent? Did we ever apologise for our mistakes, or did we need to appear perfect in order to appear superior?

Those of us who managed others looked at how we nurtured those we were responsible for and how we could encourage them, rather than bullying or criticising them. We worked on appreciating a person's good points before discussing things they could do better or differently so they were less likely to feel criticised and to be defensive and demotivated.

Some of the people on the course were from teaching and caring professions, and they came to realise how vital knowledge of self-esteem could be in their professions. The teachers said that they could see how focusing on a pupil's self-esteem could bring out the best in that pupil, because we all perform better if we feel encouraged, rather than criticised. The doctors, nurses, and carers, expressed that they felt very good at caring for the physical needs of patients, but perhaps they could do better with their patients' emotional needs. They admitted that if they had been in hospital themselves, they had felt out of control and slightly less of a person. If they could find a way to meet a person's medical needs whilst also aiming to maintain their dignity, individuality, and self-esteem, then they believed patients were likely to recover more quickly and successfully from a medical and an emotional point of view.

'What treatment in an emergency is
administered by ear? . . . Words of comfort'
—Abraham Verghese: Cutting for Stone

'When one does not know how to convince,
one oppresses; in all power relations among
governors and governed, as ability declines,
usurpation increases.'
—Madame de Stael

Outstanding leaders go out of their way to
boost the self-esteem of their personnel. If
people believe in themselves, it's amazing what
they can accomplish.
—Sam Walton

BULLYING

Bullies are classic examples of people with low self-esteem. A bully may have been bullied himself or herself or have low self-esteem for another reason. If we bully someone else, then we feel in some way inadequate and want to feel stronger and more powerful than another person so we feel better about ourselves. We usually pick what we perceive to be a weaker person and try to get power over them. We might not do this consciously; many of us do not recognise that we are bullies because we are not acknowledging the effect our behaviour has on someone else, particularly if the other person doesn't speak out or fight back.

If we are being bullied, maintaining our self-esteem can be difficult. Constant physical or emotional abuse, lack of power or control, and dealing with ridicule and criticism are among the most miserable conditions anyone can endure. It is easy to believe that the bully's view of us is right, that the negative things they say about us are true. Even if they don't outwardly abuse us, we can start to believe that the way we feel around them is a true reflection of how we actually are; that is, if we feel worthless, useless, incompetent, and weak around them, we can start to believe that we really are worthless, useless, incompetent, and weak.

Surviving and recovering from a bullying situation requires a lot of strength because we need to fight hard to regain and control our self-worth and self-confidence. It takes strength to refuse to believe what another person tells us to be true or to refuse to believe that we deserve to be treated in the way they treat us. This challenge is particularly difficult for a child; children are apt to believe what people tell them to be true, as they have not yet developed an independent view of themselves. Positive messages and emotional support from parents and teachers are vital if a child is to be able to reduce the impact of bullying on his or her self-esteem.

It is also difficult to think about the bully as a person. He or she is just 'the enemy', but evil actions don't necessarily define an evil person. Bullies act in order to feel better about themselves, and if we can have the strength to feel sorry for the bully for needing to behave badly, then the bully's influence over us will be reduced, and we can separate ourselves from them. The responsibility to change is theirs alone, but we can see bullies as people with emotional weaknesses and needs, rather than as monsters we cannot understand and from whom we cannot escape.

> 'People whose integrity has not been damaged
> in childhood . . . will feel no need to harm
> another person or themselves.'
> —Dr Alice Miller

Money

'I don't think it's a good attitude in your
life to feel that you have to be rich to have
self-esteem.'
—Tom Petty

In our society money means success because it brings status, power, and the material things we think we need or should have. The influence of money on our self-esteem can be substantial: we can feel confident and worthy with it and can feel worthless without it. This is why millions of us play the lottery; we think if we win we will be happier. But would we be?

As the song says, 'money can't buy you love.' It can't buy you self-esteem or happiness either; otherwise, all rich people would be happy, and they are not. Having money is an empty happiness because, if you have only money but nothing else of real value, then you do not have feelings of self-worth or self-confidence. Sometimes the 'richest' people in the world are financially the poorest; people who have found love, inner peace, and total acceptance of themselves and their situation are not striving for something to make them happy; they have already found happiness and contentment with who they are and what they already have.

How do you spend or control money? Do you feel better after a shopping spree, but maybe quickly have feelings of guilt? Have you ended up in debt as a result of spending too much money on things that make you feel better?

Do you argue with people about money? Arguments about money are common, and they affect us because of the emotional value we place on money. The amount of money someone spends on another person can be seen as an indication of how much the person loves the other, so money and feelings of love can quickly become intertwined.

How did your parents handle money? What did money mean in your family, and what does it mean for you now? Do you need money to feel okay? Do you always wish you had more?

'Fortune does not change men, it unmasks
them.'
—Suzanne Necker

'The trouble with the rat race is that even if
you win, you're still a rat.'
—Lily Tomlin

STRESS AND DEPRESSION

We experience stress when we perceive the demands being placed on us as exceeding our ability to cope with them. We experience lower self-confidence in that situation and often feel anxious or panicky.

Stress can lead to depression if feelings of anxiety and not being able to cope persist. Depression is a significant problem in our society, as many millions of us are on or have been on anti-depressants—and the problem seems to be getting worse. This situation indicates that experiencing feelings of low self-esteem is a widespread issue that individuals and society as a whole could well address. There are many factors in depression, and much that can cause or contribute to it, but if, with appropriate help, we could be gentler on ourselves and learn to acknowledge our own value and limitations, then we could hopefully find acceptance of ourselves and our current situation and therefore feel an increase in our self-esteem and ability to cope.

> 'Depression can seem worse than terminal
> cancer, because most cancer patients feel loved
> and they have hope and self-esteem.'
> —David D. Burns

Once we can accept ourselves, and others, as we are, then we can hopefully experience inner peace and contentment rather than feeling that life is a series of stressful events for which we may not have the ability to cope.

'Nothing seems so tragic to one who is old as
the death of one who is young, and this alone
proves that life is a good thing.'
—Zoe Atkins

"For years I have endeavoured to calm an
impetuous tide—labouring to make my
feelings take an orderly course—I was striving
against the stream"
—Mary Wollstonecraft

"Life is under no obligation to give us what
we expect"
—Margaret Mitchell

ILLNESS AND CHRONIC PAIN

Bill

It all started when I got a new job. I suddenly had much more stress at work, and although I enjoyed it at first, I quickly felt like I couldn't cope. Then I had a car accident and got signed off. I needed the rest from work, but I also had whiplash and back pain. I was signed off for six weeks, but although apparently everything was healed after this time, I still felt pain. I pursued an insurance claim against the lorry that drove into me, and I received a few thousand in compensation. This made me feel better because at least it validated how bad my injuries were and how the accident wasn't my fault. I continued to feel back and neck pain for many months after the accident. I went to all kinds of health professionals and had many types of treatments and pain killers, but nothing seemed to work for long. In the end I was told that it was all in my head! I couldn't believe they were saying this to me because, if I felt the pain, then it was real. Why would my head be creating it?

Physical illness or injury of any kind has a significant potential to affect our self-esteem, particularly if it affects our working or social lives and prevents us from doing things that would otherwise raise or maintain our self-esteem. Certain injuries or illness in certain individuals can lead to chronic pain, particularly back pain, which is one of the major problems of society and the reason that millions of working hours are lost every day. Chronic pain is a complex issue involving physical and psychological contributing factors, but an exploration of the role of self-esteem could be relevant.

Bill—a few months later

I eventually got some help from a chronic pain specialist and also came across the videos of David Butler and Lorimer Moseley on the internet. I began to realise that it really was up to me to make a choice about how I responded to the pain I was still feeling. After the accident happened, I obviously didn't like having back and neck pain, but because I didn't really understand that my body would do the healing job for me, without my intervention, I had been afraid of increasing or prolonging the pain, so I had unconsciously allowed the pain to make significant changes to the way I moved and what I did—changes that weren't really necessary. I had also unconsciously liked these changes in some ways; for instance, the financial compensation had validated and highlighted the pain I had, which unconsciously prolonged it. The time off work had a similar unconscious effect, as did the sympathy from family and friends. Gradually, my brain got the message to keep producing the pain, so the 'positive' changes were also maintained.

I learnt that the pain input to the brain from a site of injury ceases after about six weeks, in other words, once the body has healed itself. After this, the pain is termed chronic because the acute source of the pain is no longer there (unless a new injury has occurred). What often remains, however, is the brain output, which I experienced as pain and was afraid of, but if this had no actual physical cause, then I had no reason to be afraid of it! Once I realised that pain itself cannot actually harm us but that it is just an expression of something happening within our bodies—or is even the product of our brains, rather than a reality—I became much less afraid of feeling it. There are many examples of people who can control pain with their minds by removing their fear of it. They can undergo surgical operations or perform painful stunts, without any pain killers.

Once I faced my fear of the pain and decided I could overcome it, I felt so much better about myself. I had previously seen the pain as an angry red burning fire which was consuming me, but I had soon controlled it down to a small occasional irritation, just by facing it and not being afraid. My sense of self and self-esteem had become linked with being 'a person with chronic back pain', but once I disconnected the two I decided to choose for myself how I wanted my life to be: free from the fear of pain. I took it step by step with help from professionals, but I have never looked back, and today I am usually entirely pain-free. When I do feel pain, I keep the fear of it in perspective and I continue with exercise and positive activities that make me feel good.

Habits and Addictions

Sarah—too fat, too thin?

I have been overweight since I was a teenager. I can't remember a time that I wasn't teased or bullied about my weight. I hate people staring at me, and I know they are judging me, so then I eat to comfort myself, but hate myself for it. I eat when I am sad, happy, and everything in between. It makes me feel good, but then I feel worse about myself afterwards. It is a vicious circle. I can hear my mother's voice in my head criticising me and telling me to stop, but then I eat to spite her because I hate being told what to do. I have tried so many diets, and some of them work for a while, but if I get stressed for whatever reason I don't keep them up and the weight piles back on. I am worried for my own health but feel powerless to get out of the situation.

A year later.

What worked for me in the end was meeting Paula, who was anorexic. It sounds weird, but despite judging her and being unable to understand her to begin with, I soon realised that we were similar but opposite. We both used food to feel in control; she would not eat to feel in control, and I would eat to feel in control. We both had a poor body image and low self-esteem. In the end it was counselling, friendship, and shared interests that saved us both. She will always be skinny, and I will always be large—we make an odd couple—but we have found things to replace our control of food, and we have found other hobbies and interests that give us self-worth and self-confidence and that help us not to over eat or under eat. As friends, we are always there for each other if we feel judged by other people. A lot of people stare at us when we are together, but we don't care as much anymore. We have found other friends, too. Now that I feel more confident in myself, I am more confident around others.

We asked our parents to stop judging and criticising us and just to love us as we are. First they felt we were blaming them for our problems, but it wasn't about that; it was about asking for support to feel better about ourselves and to feel more in control. Once they realised we weren't blaming them, they were really supportive.

I feel proud of myself that I have come through some hard years and am now a healthy weight. Because I feel more consistently good about myself, I am more able to control the type and amount of food I eat. I eat mindfully now, rather than mindlessly, so I concentrate on enjoying the taste of food, rather than eating simply to fill an emotional hole as I was before. I eat plenty of normal, healthy, non-processed food and don't deny myself things if I really want them, but if I crave something, I ask myself whether it is for an emotional reason. I am trying not to let food be an emotional crutch anymore. I don't judge or criticise myself; I am just who I am. I do my best, and I am okay with that. I work on maintaining my self-esteem and focus on loving and appreciating those around me. The food issue is not such an issue anymore.

Belinda—cosmetic surgery

I can't help having cosmetic surgery. Each time I have a procedure, I feel much better about myself, but then I see something else that needs improving, so I arrange for something else to be done. I want to look perfect, but sometimes even I don't know what I mean by that anymore. I want to stop, but to do that I would have to accept myself as I am, and I don't know if I am strong enough to do that.

Stuart—drugs and alcohol

I didn't do well in school; I always bunked off. I started smoking when I was twelve, then I started doing pot, and then drinking and doing other drugs. I didn't see it as a problem; it was just something I did to have a good time. I got a job in a factory and got a girlfriend, but then I quit the job because my boss kept picking on me, and my girlfriend dumped me because she said I was high or drunk all the time. She said I had a problem, but I thought that she was the one with the problem because she wasn't letting me have any fun.

Looking back, I can see that she was right. I was using drugs and alcohol to escape from my life because it felt like a rubbish life and that everyone was out to get me. I finally got a grip on myself and realised that I could live without drugs or alcohol. It was a hard road, and I needed lots of help along the way to keep believing in myself, but it was worth it to be free of a life like that.

> 'Drugs are a waste of time. They destroy your memory and your self-respect and everything that goes along with your self-esteem. They're no good at all.'
> —Kurt Cobain

TEENAGERS

'I didn't have high self-esteem when I was a
teenager, as I think most teenagers don't.'
—Alanis Morisette

Bethan

*I don't get on with my mum. My parents are divorced, and I
see my dad every other weekend. It is great when I visit him
because he lets me do what I want and lets me be myself. We
watch a film, go shopping, go out for lunch, or something, and
I sometimes talk to him about stuff, or I sometimes don't.*

*My mum is always shouting at me. She hates my dad because
he left her, and we don't talk about him. My older sister has
left home, so there's just me and Mum. She's always on at me
about doing my homework, who I'm going out with, what I'm
wearing, or how much money I've spent on clothes. It doesn't
matter what I do: I'm always wrong. I don't tell her anything
now if I can help it because she'll just be cross or upset, but then
she'll find something out and be cross that I didn't tell her. I
want to change my A-level subjects but I know she won't listen.
I realise now that I chose them because my sister did them and
I wanted to prove that I could too, but I am not really good at
them and I want to change to something I can do well. There is
no way Mum will listen, though; she will just say that I should
work harder and stick with them. She says I don't love her or
respect her, but she doesn't love or respect me. She doesn't know
who I am.*

Amanda—Bethan's mother

I don't know what to do with Bethan. We were so close when she was younger, but since my divorce and her sister went to college, we just don't seem to get on anymore. I don't like who she goes out with, and I don't know if she gets her homework done or what she is going to do with her life. She tells me lies and keeps things from me, which makes me worry more and makes me angry. I try to get through to her that I care about her and want to know what she is doing and who she is with, but she just shouts and screams at me and storms off. I have decided to go for counselling so I can talk to someone.

After several weeks of counselling

Things with Bethan are much better. I have stopped criticising and shouting at her and have instead explained tearfully how much I love her and how I want her to be happy and to do well in life. I have explained my fears and why I feel worried and cross sometimes. I realise now that I wasn't accepting her just as she is; I wanted her to be how I thought she should be, rather than listening to her thoughts and aspirations.

I can see now that my divorce left me feeling bad about myself and not good enough, and my older daughter's leaving home changed things and made me focus too much on having control of Bethan. I want to be happier in myself now and am taking on new challenges at work and taking up a new hobby. I have even decided to get a new hairstyle! As I feel better about myself, I am able to be kinder and more accepting of Bethan. I think we are going to be okay now. She is a wonderful young woman, and I love her just as she is. I think she loves me more, too, now that I am a supportive mum and friend to her and have stopped being so judgmental.

Bailey

I think it's harder to be a teenager these days. Because of all the gangs and stuff, everyone thinks we are all bad. We know it is going to be hard to find a job, so a lot of us hardly see the point in school; we might as well not bother. Some people only want to get a job so they can afford alcohol or drugs and get high.

A friend of mine ended up in prison. His parents didn't care about his going to school, so he dropped out and had nothing to do and ended up joining a gang. He had to commit crimes to get in, and then they got more and more serious. He was bragging to me about how brave he was and how I should join too because he felt great about himself and important for once. When he came out of prison, he knew there was even less chance he would ever get a regular job, so he just carried on like before. There was no one who believed in him or who might help him to change.

I think some people think criminals are evil people, but I don't think they are. My friend just chose crime to feel powerful and better about himself; it was the only way he could see to improve his life, to 'be someone' and get noticed. He had to be punished for what he did, but I don't think prison works. He came out of there more convinced than ever that crime was his only option. I know he was assaulted and abused in prison, but he doesn't talk about it; instead, he has become even 'harder' and is more involved in gangs and drugs than ever. I don't think anything could change him now unless he wanted to change himself, and even then it would be difficult. There are so many people like him that I think something needs to be done. Nobody seems to believe in young people anymore, especially if they make stupid mistakes because they are just trying to make themselves feel better.

Self-harm and Suicide

Catriona

I have being cutting myself since I was twelve. My mum is an alcoholic and my dad left when I was five. I've been in foster homes, but I'm back with my mum now. Cutting myself makes me feel good. I feel a release from everything else around me, but then afterwards I feel empty again and disappointed with myself, and I can't look at what I have done to my body. No one understands why I do it. Sometimes I can stop for a few weeks, but then I get picked on at school or something and I start again. I tried to kill myself last year with tablets. I don't have anything to live for, and nobody would care if I wasn't here.

Twelve months later

I've been seeing a counsellor, and I'm starting to feel a bit better about myself. I used to feel totally useless and unwanted, and I still do a bit, but I am starting to see that I am good at some things, and just because my parents haven't been around for me, it doesn't mean that other people won't be there for me. I can be there for myself as well; I'm pretty strong to have gone through the things I have done. I still want people to care about me, but I am realising that I am going to have to care about myself first. I am doing a bit better in school, particularly in English. I like the teacher and she thinks I should stay on and do the A-level. I think I would like to be a teacher because she has believed in me, and I would like to do that for someone else in a situation like mine. I haven't cut myself for a few months now. Sometimes I want to, but I get past the feeling by doing something else, such as homework, helping my mum, or getting out of the house and seeing a friend. I am getting on better with my mum. She isn't in a great place, but I am trying to help her to feel better about herself. She is going to AA meetings and might go for counselling as well.

Darren

I have tried to commit suicide a couple of times now. I am divorced, and my girlfriend has dumped me, too. I have a dead-end job and nothing to live for. I have two boys, but they live with their mum and her new husband; they don't need me. My ex-wife doesn't even let me in the house; she says she would prefer not to see me at all. I hate her. Why has all this happened to me? Why has my life turned out like this? What have I done to deserve it? I'm going to make sure I commit suicide properly next time so that all this is over.

Twelve months later

I can't believe how I felt back then. I can remember feeling that way, but I was being so selfish that I am embarrassed now. I have lived my whole life as if I am not responsible for my actions and not responsible for the relationships in my life, and now I realise that only I am responsible for my own happiness. My girlfriend eventually got through to me, and we are back together now. She made me realise that suicide would have devastated the lives of my family and friends, especially my parents and children. What might they have believed about themselves if they had a son/father who killed himself? How would they have felt? It might have affected their self-esteem for the rest of their lives. My ex-wife would have been traumatised, too. I don't hate her. I see now how bad our marriage was for both of us, but if I had killed myself, I would have been selfishly *making her life even more difficult. She would have had two grieving children, and she might have felt guilty for the rest of her life, even though it was me, not her, who was responsible for killing myself.*

My girlfriend has been amazing, I didn't deserve her back then. For a long time I was just using her to feel better about myself. I was begging her to need me and to love me, and I was becoming abusive and jealous if it seemed like she didn't love me enough. No wonder she dumped me. Now I realise that love is about being there for the other person. I focus on making sure I am there to support her and to make her feel loved just for who she is. I am starting to believe I do deserve her, as long as I can be the best person I can be, rather than the self-centred idiot I was before. I am trying to re-build things with my children. As long as I work on my own self-esteem first, I know I will get there with them, and they will see that they can trust me and that I will always be there for them. How could I have thought of suicide and not have had the chance to be there for them and to see them grow up?

Social Networking

Micheal

I lost my smart phone last week, and that was when I realised I am addicted to social networking, texting, and generally playing on my phone. I felt shaky, worried all the time, and not myself at all, as if I had physically lost a piece of my body. I couldn't think about anything other than where my phone might be and about needing it back. I felt cut off, isolated, and worthless because I couldn't connect with anyone or see what my friends were up to. I couldn't even let them know that I had lost my phone.

My phone turned up the next day, but once I had it back, I felt different about it because I realised how addicted I had become. I was surprised by how shaken I had been, not just because of its financial value but because I had felt cut off from the world. And then I thought, how sad is that?

I realised how many hours of the day I spend on the internet 'talking' to people but not actually talking face-to-face to anyone at all. I feel like I exist only when I am online, and I am sure lots of my friends feel the same; it is like they can't enjoy something unless they immediately tell everyone online about it. I didn't ever think I would call myself an addict of anything, but I am a social networking addict. I use it to escape when I am down, to celebrate when I am up, and for pretty much everything in between. I feel like I cannot survive without it, and I don't think this feeling is healthy for me.

I used to value lots of other things, like just sitting and talking to people and really focussing on what they were saying, or sitting in the sunshine and daydreaming. I don't daydream anymore! I have decided to switch my phone off more often, like when I want to think about something or when I am having a meal or a drink with people, and I might even try leaving my phone at home sometimes when I am out with my girlfriend. She should feel that she is worth my full attention.

Has our self-esteem become caught up in our ability to gain feedback and validity from others via social networking sites? We can 'tweet' or change our Facebook status instantly, which broadcasts our thoughts or actions to hundreds or thousands of people. Their reactions might support or condemn us, and based on these reactions, we might feel good or bad about ourselves. Have we lost some of the control over our own self-worth and self-confidence because it is so easy to seek the instant opinions of others? Have the opinions of virtual strangers started to matter more than the opinions we have of ourselves?

Retirement

Margaret

I think we had a good marriage until my husband retired. Since then, he has struggled to find something to replace work. I think he feels a bit useless now and not as valued or as confident. He seems to resent that I am okay and still meet my friends for coffee or to go out in the evening to meetings or the theatre. He doesn't like it when I'm not in the house, but he doesn't talk to me or want to do much together when I am around. It feels like our happy marriage has drifted away.

I try to help him to be positive; I ask him to come with me to things or suggest things that he might like to do, but this doesn't seem to help because he thinks I am nagging. He criticises me about lots of things and accuses me of doing or saying things which I would never do or say. I think he might be struggling with feeling physically and mentally older and not as capable of doing everything he used to do when he was younger. He seems more fearful of things now that wouldn't have bothered him before. I want to help him, but I don't know how. I want him to want to help himself.

I don't think he would ever agree to see a counsellor, but perhaps I can admit to him that I feel less capable and more fearful sometimes, too, and that I would like him to help me to feel more positive. Perhaps, if he knows I need him, it will make him feel more valued and he will want to take more interest in himself. Whatever he does, I am not going to take it personally any more. I was starting to worry that it was me who had caused him to be like this somehow—that it was my fault—but only he can change how he chooses to see himself and how he lives his life. I am going to do my best to help him for as long as I can because I am strong enough now to see that he isn't trying to put me down when he criticises me; he is just trying to feel better about himself.

Spirituality, Religion, and Silence

Jeff

I have struggled with the question of whether I believe in God for years. I have tried several religions and denominations and have just become confused about whether there is one I should believe in. Someone said to me that they didn't believe a person could find true self-worth without a spiritual element—that we can't do it on our own but must have faith in God in order to achieve inner peace, forgiveness, and self-worth. I can see the logic in this because a person who has a strong faith and belief is very likely to feel more at peace with themselves. Faith in God must bring comfort and security because you know you are loved by God and are not alone. There must be a sense of belonging when others believe the same as you do.

The problem as I see it, though, is that there are thousands of religions and beliefs, and I don't understand how one can be 'right' and the others 'wrong'. I think that faith can give an individual the self-worth and self-confidence they are seeking, which is a good thing, but it might also lead them to judge others as being 'wrong' because they have a different faith. All too often, religious faith seems to lead people to criticise and judge each other, which is surely the opposite of acknowledging every individual's equal worth as a human being. I'm sure, if there is a God, that He wants unity in our world, not division.

I feel that, at last, I am finding inner self-worth and confidence without belief in a specific religion or ideology. I came across the BBC series, The Big Silence, and found it fascinating. Five individuals were challenged to spend eight days in silence at a retreat centre. Most of us would find this extremely strange and difficult because, in our fast-paced, modern world, we seldom experience silence. Religions and spirituality almost always include elements of silence, usually in order to communicate with God, but also to communicate with ourselves and our inner thoughts and feelings. The individuals in the program took a long time to settle into really experiencing silence, and they went through extreme and varied emotions when they did so because they were forced to face their inner selves without being distracted from their own uncomfortable or unwelcome thoughts. Some of them found God, and some of them simply found themselves. In our fast-paced, modern world, we seldom ever experience silence, which seems to imply that our 'happiness' usually needs to involve noise. Do we constantly distract ourselves in case silence will make us feel unhappy? I also came across the poem 'Desiderata' by Max Ehrmann, which sums up my feelings. I read it frequently now to help me navigate life.

When did you last spend time sitting in total silence, doing nothing? How would you feel if you spent days sitting somewhere, with no verbal contact from anyone else and nothing to do? Avoiding being alone with our thoughts can be a sign that we carry feelings of low self-esteem or not being okay with just ourselves. If we can practice sitting in silence and feeling a sense of love for ourselves and value in our lives, then we will be making a good start to increasing our own self-esteem. Only you can give yourself the gift of time to sit in silence and the time to find the gift of inner self-worth. If we can be alone with our thoughts and feel comfortable, then we are at ease with ourselves and who we are.

> 'Concentrate on silence. When it comes, dwell
> on what it sounds like.
> Then strive to carry that quiet with you
> wherever you go.'
> —Paul Wilson, *The Little Book of Calm*

Mindfulness

'Most worries are future-based. They revolve
around things that, in most cases, will never
happen. Concentrate on the present and the
future will take care of itself.'
—Paul Wilson, *The Little Book of Calm*

Mindfulness describes the act of paying attention to
the present, rather than letting our minds wander to the
problems of the past, or the worries of the future. We can
always feel okay in the present because, moment by moment,
we can choose to be content with who we are and where we
are, even if it is not where we might choose to be. Once
we are content, it is easier to find positivity and pleasure
in what is around us, and we can focus on appreciating the
people in our lives there and then.

If we find it difficult to appreciate each day, moment by
moment, we can learn to analyse where our self-esteem is taking
us and what past or future threat is distracting us from enjoying
the present. As we become faster at analysing our feelings, we
can more easily concentrate on enjoying the present and allow
future worries to take care of themselves at the appropriate time.
It isn't always easy, but with gentle practice, it is possible.

'When you concentrate your attention
on absorbing every detail of every
moment—savouring every taste, hearing every
sound, noting every colour—you will be calm
before you know it.'
—Paul Wilson, *The Little Book of Calm*

Nature or Nurture

Many have debated whether nature or nurture plays the greater role in our development, and I find myself wondering whether our ability to take charge of our self-esteem and to feel okay about ourselves and others, is influenced more by nature or by nurture.

Could self-esteem be something for which we are born with a natural affinity, or do we learn it through nurturing as a young child? It is likely to be both, but people who seem to be on an unstoppable path of self-destruction, despite love from others who are trying to help build their self-esteem, make me wonder whether our inherent nature could sometimes be one of low self-esteem and whether there is little such people can do about it.

Imagine two children who experience similar critical, unloving, or abusive childhoods. Both find something they are good at, and people who value them and care about them. One child might come to recognise his or her own self-worth and find self-confidence, while the other one, despite similar opportunities and achievements, might, tragically, always feel inadequate and unlovable.

The kindest people in life are often those who have experienced kindness and unconditional love in their upbringing, but some individuals, despite loving and non-critical people around them, might still have found reasons in their childhood or adolescence to think badly of themselves, and to be critical and abusive to others.

Sometimes the kindest people can actually be those who have experienced a lot of criticism and abuse in their childhoods, they somehow find a way to reject such an unkind way of being and to show themselves and others the love and acceptance they didn't experience as children or young adults.

No one can give us self-esteem, so it is true that we can only change ourselves and not other people. I hope that we can all learn, if we haven't already, to accept ourselves as good enough, rather than being overly self-critical or trying to be perfect, and that we can stop criticising others (if we do), and go on to live a happy life in which we are kind to others and to ourselves.

THE MEANING OF LIFE

If I had to describe the meaning of life, I would say something like this:

The meaning of life is to appreciate, value, and love the bodies and minds we are given at birth and to value our own uniqueness and the attributes we naturally possess; to appreciate and value the uniqueness of others and their attributes; to help others value themselves by showing them acceptance and unconditional love; to try to create peace and harmony in the world, starting with ourselves, and to try to help the self- esteem of those around us by showing them acceptance and love.

If all of us did this, then maybe, little by little, we could achieve the impossible dream for which the Miss World contestants always wish: world peace!

'Our prime purpose in this life is to help others.
And if you can't help them, at least don't hurt them.'
—Dalai Lama

'World peace begins with inner peace.'
—Dalai Lama

'Every nation is convinced that she is dedicated to peace, but that the actions of other nations are open to suspicion. Every system of government is warranted by its

upholders to ensure harmonious relations,
while every other system must lead inevitably
to war.'
—Agnes Reppler

Kindness and the Big Society

How kind are we to each other? Some people are consistently kind, non-critical, and thoughtful, and it is these people who have the greatest control over their self-esteem. They have found the way to accept others as they are and not to allow people, events, or circumstances to change how they choose to conduct themselves. Kind people find a way, often in spite of difficult circumstances, to show understanding and appreciation of others. Consistently kind people are both strong and rare; while we could all be like them if we chose to be, it takes an individual decision to work on changing ourselves.

> 'Prejudices, it is well known, are most difficult
> to eradicate from the heart whose soil has
> never been loosened or fertilized by education;
> they grow firm there, firm as weeds among
> stones.'
> —Charlotte Bronte

Not everyone wants to be kind; some people consider it a sign of weakness to be kind to their 'enemies' and those they judge as inferior in some way, but showing kindness is the greatest form of strength. We can choose to behave in a kind, moral, and considerate way, no matter what anyone else does. If more of us were kinder and more understanding, our communities, towns, cities, countries, and the world would be better places to live.

'You can't shake hands with a clenched fist.'
—Indira Ghandi

The current UK government talks about the 'Big Society'. What I would love to see is a world that came together street by street, village by village, town by town, city by city, and country by country with a common purpose of increasing our collective self-esteem so that we become kinder and more considerate as human beings, and show positive traits of strength, rather than aggression and division, which are signs of weakness.

'To suffer is to be alone; to watch another suffer is to know the barrier that shuts each of us away. Only individuals can suffer.'
—Edith Hamilton

I wish it were easy to give feelings of self-esteem to children, young people, and the adults they become. If we could, many of society's problems would disappear because kind, confident people tend to choose positive, rather than destructive, ways to behave. Even on an international level, nations fight other nations and governments or dictators fight their own people often in order to feel powerful and prove their own importance. This is a tragedy; their need to feel 'strength' comes at a terrible price.

'Nearly all men can stand adversity, but if you want to test a man's character, give him power.'
—Abraham Lincoln

Self-esteem cannot be given by someone else; we each have to find it for ourselves. But wouldn't it be good to live in a society where it was the responsibility of all to help each other feel more positive about ourselves and others? Attempting to control and reduce antisocial, violent, and criminal behaviour via condemnation and punishment isn't working very well. Maybe there is another way.

> 'Never doubt that a small group of thoughtful,
> committed people can change the world.
> Indeed, it is the only thing that ever has.'
> —Margaret Mead

Once a year, on World Kindness Day, we are encouraged to think about being kind to others. Shouldn't World Kindness Day be every day?

> 'Ask yourself: Have you been kind today?
> Make kindness your daily modus operandi
> and change your world.'
> —Annie Lennox

> It is one of the most beautiful compensations
> of life that no man can sincerely try
> to help another without helping himself'
> —Ralph Waldo Emerson

> 'I think the biggest disease the world suffers
> from in this day and age is the disease of
> people feeling unloved. I know that I can give

love for a minute, for half an hour, for a day,
for a month, but I can give. I am very happy
to do that, I want to do that.'
—Princess Diana

DEDICATION

I dedicate this book to anyone who experiences trauma in their lives and manages to carry on with bravery and kindness to themselves and others. I have had the privilege of meeting clients who are incredible people, and I have inspirational family members and friends who support me, but I specifically dedicate this book to the partners and families of the armed forces personnel, past and present, because their courage and strength is often not understood, and usually goes unnoticed and unrewarded.

The partners of armed forces personnel usually endure frequent house moves, often at short notice, sometimes on their own, and probably to an unexpected place or an unfamiliar country. They have no choice in where they live or how long it might take to have quarters allocated to them. They repeatedly go through the process of leaving friends and making new ones, the worry of finding schools for children, sometimes only days before a new term begins or in the middle of one, and the process of trying to find a job, if they want one. Our armed forces partners cope repeatedly, at short-notice, and often for months on end, with being alone. They are often isolated from family and friends and might frequently have to face the fear of knowing their loved one is in danger in a war zone and might come back seriously injured—or not at all. Some might think that an armed forces partner knew what they were getting into and what they would have to cope with, but it is impossible to know what living as a partner in the armed forces is like until you experience it. Armed forces partners need to become experts at finding ways to remain calm and to maintain their belief in themselves, no matter what challenge each new day brings; and then to pass these skills on to their children.

Some of the Army, Navy and RAF wives I have lived alongside over the past eight years have displayed an incredible ability to stay calm and content no matter what life has thrown at them. I have the greatest admiration for the way they have coped with constant change and difficulties, and yet remained happily married and loving parents, who are true to themselves. They have been inspirational to me.

Final Words

Someone said to me recently that if all we do in a day is show kindness and love to ourselves and those around us, then we will have achieved more that day than some people manage in a lifetime. The jobs, challenges, and tasks of life will always be there, but you and the people in your life, will not.

Printed in the United States
By Bookmasters